Contents

Contents

Part 1

Introduction

The author

William Shakespeare was baptised in Stratford-on-Avon on 26 April, 1564. His father, John Shakespeare, was a merchant and tradesman of that country market town, while his mother came of the family of Arden who had been landowners in Warwickshire for many years. John Shakespeare seems to have enjoyed increasing prosperity and success until 1668 when he became bailiff of the town, but what records we have suggest that, after that, legal, financial, and possibly religious troubles brought harsher times to the family.

We know nothing certain about Shakespeare's childhood and education, but he most probably attended a local grammar school where the standard of teaching was reasonably high. Towards the end of 1582 he married a local girl, Anne Hathaway of Whateley and the following May a daughter, Susanna, was baptised. In February 1585 the baptism of twins, Hamnet and Judith, is recorded.

Despite many detailed theories we know nothing of Shakespeare's life between the birth of the twins and the attack launched on his character and writings by the dying Robert Greene in London in 1592, an attack which makes it clear that Shakespeare was by that time an actor (or 'player' as they were usually known), and a writer of plays which had already gained some popular success.

During his successful London years Shakespeare kept his roots in his native town. It seems most likely that his wife and children stayed there all the time (Hamnet, his only son, was buried in Stratford in August 1596). In 1597 Shakespeare bought New Place, a large house in the town, and, at other times, various local properties. It is probable that about 1610 he left London and retired permanently to his Stratford home where he died on St George's Day (April 23) 1616. He is buried in the church there. Both of his daughters married, but his direct descendants have died out.

When we examine the many theories which claim that William Shakespeare of Stratford-on-Avon could not have written the plays and poems which go under his name, we find that the persistent silliness of the theorists is rooted in two circumstances: first, in the secrecy of Shakespeare's inner life—except for the enigmatic *Sonnets*, no great writer seems less autobiographical; secondly in the social and cultural snobbery which refuses to accept that the son of a small-town tradesman could be one of the very greatest writers the world has ever known. As to the first of these: secrets always breed guesses; so, baffled by the personal silence of Shakespeare and excited by his work, people are bound to go on inventing Shakespeare either under other names or indeed under his own. As to the second, whoever wrote the works of Shakespeare was a genius of that kind which cannot be either explained or discounted in terms of any social, cultural, or educational background. It is just as likely or unlikely that such a phenomenon should start life in a ditch as in a palace. Finally and factually it should be said that there is a mass of varied evidence from Shakespeare's own times that he is the author, and not one shred of fact pointing clearly to any other origin.

Shakespeare and the players

At the time that Shakespeare was establishing himself in the world of the theatre the players' companies were going through a complicated process of evolution. Plays were increasingly popular in sixteenth-century England, and during the reign of Elizabeth I there began that flowering of theatre and drama which continued into the reign of James I, and which proved one of the greatest creative periods in the history of literature.

The players were formed into companies. Some of the actors were 'sharers' who owned the company and its property, and, when this property included a theatre, they might also be 'housekeepers' owning a share in the building. The rest of the company were actors and others in the employ of the sharers. Unless they were both fortunate and successful, the life of the actors was restless and uncertain, for, despite their general popularity, their activities in and around London were opposed in every possible way by the Lord Mayor and Aldermen of the city, who saw plays and playgoing as the occasions of vice, foolishness, infection, and, worst of all, distraction from an honest day's work. It was only the protection of the court that saved the players from the local authorities. Under the law they were 'vagabonds', liable to arrest unless they were under the protection of some great man and officially registered as his servants. So we find the different companies under the names of their protectors: the Admiral's men, Lord Strange's men, Leicester's men, and so on. In return for protection the players entertained their patron on demand. They also gave performances at court.

Plays for the London public were performed first in the enclosed courtyards of the inns; but these were largely replaced during the 1590s by the new playhouses which were built on an inn-yard pattern, outside the walls of the city to escape the regulations of the city authorities. When the death rate in and around London from the rat-carried bubonic plague rose above a certain level, as it did every few years, the play-houses were closed down and there were no court performances. Then the London-based players' companies took to the roads, like those lesser companies which toured most of the time, and wandered England from town to town picking up a living by local performances.

The early 1590s, when we first hear of Shakespeare the player, were hit hard by the plague. Players' companies collapsed and amalgamated in confusing combinations. Out of the confusion two main companies emerge in the mid-nineties: the Admiral's men, and the Lord Chamber-lain's men who were under the protection of Lord Hunsdon, near cousin and favoured confidant of the Queen. This second company was the one to which Shakespeare belonged.

Plays, though popular, were not considered an important form of literature, but Shakespeare made his social and literary reputation with his two long poems, written probably while the theatres were closed and both dedicated to the young Earl of Southampton. There is a tradi-tion that Southampton rewarded him with a present of money, but, wherever Shakespeare got the means, he bought a share in the Lord Chamberlain's men. He remained one of their senior members and their principal playwright for the rest of Elizabeth's reign while they became the premier company and court favourites, and for the first seven years or so of the reign of James I while they maintained their success and became 'The King's Men'. Marks of the success of the company were the building of their own playhouse, The Globe, opened on Bankside in 1599, and the acquisition in 1608 of the lease of the Blackfriars, probably the best indoor theatre in London.

Plays and playhouses

Most great cultural movements have been the result of a strong inter-action between a local tradition and an exciting influence from outside that tradition. The English Renaissance flowering in poetry and drama is no exception, and the works of Shakespeare bear witness to the creative interaction of the great Renaissance interest in Greek and Roman literature on the one hand; and on the other to a powerful native literary tradition whose drama was rooted in the mystery and miracle plays of the Middle Ages. Plays of all sorts, 'tragedy, comedy, history, pastoral, pastoral-comical, historical-pastoral, tragical-histor-ical, tragical-comical-historical-pastoral' as Polonius says in Hamlet, were written for a public ever eager for new entertainment. When Shakespeare started, these plays were being written by a group of men with university training who sold their plays to the players' companies.

The complaint of Robert Greene, one of these 'wits', is to his fellows in the play-writing trade: he warns them against the ungrateful players who owe everything to the writers but who have abandoned him and will do the same to them; particularly now that they have their own playwright, an upstart actor, an absolute Jack-of-all-trades, who thinks he can write a play as well as anyone in the land and who steals their poetic and dramatic material. We know that this player-playwright is the young Shakespeare because Green calls him 'Shake-scene' and misquotes a line from Shakespeare's *Henry VI, Part 3*.

We also know that the players were very proud of 'their' Shakespeare, the actor who could write better than any of those learned authors. After his death it was two of his old company, John Heminges and Henry Condell, who collected and published his plays in the First Folio, where incidentally we find the earliest known printing of *Julius Caesar*.

Once a play was sold by the writer to a company it was the absolute property of that company. The players guarded their copies, particularly of popular plays, very jealously, because if they became public there was no law to prevent their performance by another company. If a play were stolen and printed the company which owned it might get some of the money of the book-buying public by bringing out their own edition of the play and thus competing with the stolen edition. In very bad times, as when the plague closed the theatres for a long period, a company might raise money by selling some of their plays to be printed. Nineteen of Shakespeare's plays were published as Quartos before the collected works of the First Folio, containing thirty-six of his plays in all, was published in 1623.

So we see that the companies owned the plays and indeed the writers did not make much from them, though payments of, say, five or seven pounds for a three-hour play are not as startlingly mean as they sound today. Shakespeare did not make his fortune directly from his plays but from his share in a successful company. However, the success of that company was due in no small measure to his plays which were popular in city and court alike.

The Elizabethan drama was conditioned by the theatre buildings, the conventions of acting and action, and the taste and expectations of a lively and varied audience. All these worked together in varying combination to determine its character. Based on the inns of the time, the theatres were built around a yard which was open to the sky. In the Fortune Theatre, which copied the Globe of Shakespeare's company, there were three storeys of galleries opening on the yard. The outer stage, overshadowed by a projecting high canopy, filled almost half the yard and backed on to an inner stage of several storeys, in which there were rooms which could be opened or closed for indoor scenes. The poorest of the audience, 'the groundlings', occupied the rest of the yard in front of, and even around the sides of the stage. Better-off folk were ranged round in the galleries, parts of which were closed off into rooms for private parties (the equivalent of modern boxes). Some of the audience even hired stools and sat on the stage itself. This then was a close-contact theatre with the audience crowded round and piled high on three sides of the stage. Models and architectural drawings, though useful, do not give a proper sense of intimacy of a performance, which is best realised in some small modern experimental theatres, or by watching the beginning of Laurence Olivier's film of *Henry V*.

THE GLOBE PLAYHOUSE

The theatre, originally built by James Burbage in 1576, was made of wood (Burbage had been trained as a carpenter). It was situated to the north of the River Thames on Shoreditch in Finsbury Fields. There was trouble with the lease of the land, and so the theatre was dismantled in 1598, and reconstructed 'in another forme' on the south side of the Thames as the Globe. Its sign is thought to have been a figure of the Greek hero Hercules carrying the globe. It was built in six months, its galleries being roofed with thatch. This caught fire in 1613 when some smouldering wadding, from a cannon used in a performance of Shakespeare's *Henry VIII*, lodged in it. The theatre was burnt down, and when it was rebuilt again on the old foundations, the galleries were roofed with tiles.

The key quality of intimacy, of the audience being *with* the actors must have also been greatly increased by the fact that the plays were acted in the great theatres in daylight. Everyone could see everyone else quite clearly. The audience were not wrapped away from the actors in darkness.

There was no attempt to try to make time, place, and weather realistically present to the audience. These things were indicated by speech or by conventional sign or action. Brutus in his orchard at night would be on the open front stage in broad daylight. See how quickly he lets the audience know that it is very late at night:

BRUTUS: What, Lucius, Ho!
        I cannot by the progress of the stars,
        Give guess how near to day.

One or two conventional stage 'trees' brought onto the front stage before the scene might tell the audience that they were in the orchard garden. Those not listening very carefully to Brutus would be helped to know the time by the constant references to tapers, sleep, darkness, bed, night, meteors and so on throughout the scene. The most spectacular visual feature of the performances was the costume of the actors which was splendid and picturesque. There was little attempt to reproduce the costume of past periods. In *Julius Caesar* there is plenty of evidence that the actors were dressed essentially as Elizabethans; but, as Granville Barker says in his excellent preface to the play, there is also evidence of some exotic touches to show that these were 'Romans'. It should be emphasised that the impression was one of heightened everyday reality.

This phrase will also give us the clue to the acting which was both as everyday and as emphatic as the costumes. The colour and excitement of Shakespeare's language is rooted firmly in everyday language and in everyday experience while at the same time being a more intense and more complete use of words. In Shakespeare's England there seems to have been a relish for effective language, and for striking mood and feeling, and the playwrights and actors responded by passionate and emphatic language and performance. The characteristic fault of the day was over-acting, 'tearing a passion to tatters' as Shakespeare disapprovingly calls it in *Hamlet*.

Before leaving this very brief glance at how the theatre of the time conditioned the plays that were written for it, some further conventions of performance and understanding should be remembered. First (not particularly significant for the very masculine *Julius Caesar*) is the fact that the female parts were all acted by boys, and however consciously or unconsciously, Shakespeare seems to have catered for what the boy actors could manage by giving them spirited, often argumentative girls

A CONJECTURAL RECONSTRUCTION OF THE INTERIOR OF
THE GLOBE PLAYHOUSE

AA Main entrance
 B The Yard
CC Entrances to lowest gallery
 D Entrance to staircase and upper galleries
 E Corridor serving the different sections of the
   middle gallery
 F Middle gallery ('Twopenny Rooms')
 G 'Gentlemen's Rooms' or Lords' Rooms'
 H The stage
 J The hanging being put up round the stage
 K The 'Hell' under the stage
 L The stage trap, leading down to the Hell
MM Stage doors

 N Curtained 'place behind the stage'
 O Gallery above the stage, used as required
   sometimes by musicians, sometimes by
   spectators, and often as part of the play
 P Back-stage area (the tiring-house)
 Q Tiring-house door
 R Dressing-rooms
 S Wardrobe and storage
 T The hut housing the machine for lowering
   enthroned gods, etc., to the stage
 U The 'Heavens'
 W Hoisting the playhouse flag

and women to portray. Both Portia and Calphurnia are made into opponents of their husbands' conduct.

Second, to return again to the flexibility of space and time on Shakespeare's stage: the fact that simply by speaking of place and hour the actor could create it, meant a possible flow, a continuity of action lost to the later theatre during that period when the curtain was lowered and the scenery and lighting changed for every scene. The strong current of events moves in *Julius Caesar* with a continuous though varied flow which would have no pause on the stage of the Globe. We shall comment later on various ways in which Shakespeare controls and imposes patterns on this flow of dramatic time and action.

There is no space to list the conventions of action, appearance and speech which we know existed in Shakespeare's theatre, we can only give some examples. There were conventions of movement, which link with what we have said of place and time, as when by walking in conversation around the stage players could get to 'another place'. There were many conventions of appearance, in that characters could be formally identified by special clothes or stage props. The colour or fashion of costume often established both a character's nationality and whether he was good or bad. There were sheets for ghosts, magic 'invisible' robes for enchanters and so on. All a man had to do to become completely unrecognisable was to do as the conspirators do: muffle his chin in his cloak and pull his hat down over his eyes.

Of the conventions of speech the soliloquy and the aside should be mentioned. An aside is always meant to be overheard by the audience and sometimes by other characters on the stage. This could be easily made clear by gesture, probably speaking behind a hand. On the English stage there was a convention, going back into the Middle Ages, of characters talking directly to the audience. In Shakespeare's plays he seems to be moving away from this to a situation where, particularly in the soliloquy, the audience are not so much addressed as 'allowed to overhear' what the dramatic character is 'thinking'. The direct chat with the audience seems to have lasted longest, even with Shakespeare, as a characteristic of villains (usually explaining their evil thoughts and plans) and of minor, usually comic characters. It is easier to think of Cassius in his early 'villain' phase, talking directly to the audience at the end of Act I, Scene 2, than to see Brutus in the orchard doing the same thing; Brutus is 'thinking', not telling us his plans.

The place of *Julius Caesar*

By 1599 Shakespeare had passed through the apprenticeship of the early plays and the assured achievement of the middle comedies and histories. *Julius Caesar* is connected closely to the histories in theme and treatment. It is moreover the first of the true tragedies. Also it is one of the Roman plays, which have special characteristics of their own. Finally many critics have included it in what have been called Shakespeare's problem plays, a group of works of the early tragic period which present special difficulties of tone and interpretation.

Just before writing *Julius Caesar* Shakespeare had finished his second cycle of history plays. These cycles were interconnected and both drawn from fairly recent English history. In them, and in the independent play *King John* which dealt with an earlier period, Shakespeare had shown himself increasingly concerned with certain tensions between the individual and public affairs which he turned to excellent dramatic use. To simplify, we may say that in these plays there is a struggle in the minds of men between ambition and conscience; according as their will is ruled by the desire for power and greatness on the one hand, and the concern for justice, order, and the common good on the other. Because of the medieval concept of kingship and hierarchy which still had power in Shakespeare's day, it is not surprising that the figure of the monarch, the king, the absolute ruler should fill the centre of his stage. It was 'upon the King' that the fortunes of the whole people depended. Good kings, bad kings; strong kings and weak ones; rightful rulers and usurpers—the histories show them all and their influence on the lives of men all down through the social order. England had known almost a century of fairly stable rule under the Tudors, but the terrible memories of prolonged civil war still disturbed the minds and hearts of men, particularly as the childless Elizabeth's reign drew to a close. How justified were these fears is proved by such events as the unsuccessful rebellion of the Earl of Essex and his friends, who to the Elizabethan audience must have born a striking resemblance to Brutus and his fellow conspirators.

Julius Caesar is one of Shakespeare's greatest histories because in it he deals powerfully and excitingly with the themes of power and conscience. It is the first of the great tragedies because in it the inner conflict and catastrophe, the individual destiny, becomes even more compelling than the public events. Of the two earlier tragedies *Titus Andronicus* is mere sensationalism almost entirely lacking in any insight into, or sympathy with, the human being in extremity; *Romeo and Juliet*, on the other hand, is a deeply moving success, but it is a *romantic* tragedy lacking that sense of awe and terror which marks the great tragedies.

Shakespeare was a dramatist who always relied heavily on the chosen sources of his plots. In his English history plays his most constant companion was Holinshed's *Chronicles*; now, turning to Roman history at the height of his powers the book he most heavily relied on was Sir Thomas North's translation of a French version of *Plutarch's Lives of the Noble Grecians and Romans*. The *Lives* contains studies of Caesar, Brutus and Anthony; and Shakespeare follows these very closely indeed, often using the very words of his source. Later we shall consider some of the changes he made in order to try to understand better his dramatic method and intention.

Julius Caesar, recognised as one of the greatest men the world had ever known, was a daunting subject for any writer, particularly since it called for a mind ready to challenge the Greek and Roman authors on their own ground. The influence and rivalry of Shakespeare's friend Ben Jonson, a profound and passionate classicist, may well have led to Shakespeare's choice of subject and certainly must have added competitive zest to the enterprise. Jonson had faults to find with Shakespeare's play, but his own later efforts to write Roman tragedies, *Catiline* and *Sejanus*, though far more 'correct' according to neo-classical rules of drama, are dull and heavy. Indeed there is evidence that Shakespeare himself made far greater efforts to be 'correct' in writing his first great Roman play than he did in almost any other of his works. As we shall see when we consider the structure of the play, it bears all the marks of the most careful, almost mechanical, composition, and such critics as Dr Johnson and Granville-Barker have also said that in making his Romans noble Shakespeare has made them somewhat inhuman.

Another reason for turning to Rome was a new law forbidding works on English history. One peculiar advantage that Shakespeare took of the Roman setting, not only in this play but also later, in *Antony and Cleopatra* and in *Coriolanus*, was his use of a pagan world as a morally neutral ground. It may be said that in these plays he refuses to judge the character and actions of his people in the same way as he does in most of his other plays. The moral world of *Julius Caesar* is deeply ambiguous, and the sympathy of a spontaneous audience shifts about from Caesar to Pompey, to Brutus, to Caesar, back to Brutus, to Antony, to Cassius, back to Brutus, to Cassius, to Brutus again; and finally to a kind of reconciliation, after the death of Brutus. This shifting sympathy gives the play certain sorts of strength and also certain weaknesses. It is a powerfully realistic vision of the world of power politics where there are seldom any really clear-cut black-and-white judgements to be made. On the other hand it deprives the play of a psychological centre of sympathy to the extent that we may say that this is a tragedy without a real hero, a real central protagonist. Why is the play called *Julius Caesar* if it is the tragedy of Brutus? If it is the tragedy of Caesar, whoever heard of a great tragedy whose hero dies half-way through?

The moral and emotional ambiguity of the play links it also to the histories on the one hand (*Richard II* has something of the same shifting effect) and to the so-called problem plays on the other. About 1600 the mood of much English writing became bitter and satiric, and Shakespeare played his part in this change of tone. Both his tragedies and comedies for three or four years following *Julius Caesar* are marked by disillusionment and disgust with the very nature of humanity. There is very little of this darker side of Shakespeare's mind in *Julius Caesar*, very little of the disgust and sense of evil that we feel in *Hamlet*, his next tragedy; but here and there the imagery of sickness, or corruption, of weariness is heard as a countermusic to the energetic and generous language that is more characteristic of the play as a whole.

A note on the text

We have only one text for Julius Caesar, the First Folio, that collection of Shakespeare's plays published by his fellow players in 1623. It has been guessed that the printers were working from a good correct play-house promptbook because of the plentiful and useful stage directions and the remarkable freedom from mistakes and muddles of the kind all too common in the printing of many of Shakespeare's other plays. It is perhaps the best text we have of any Shakespearean play.

We can date the play with some real certainty to 1599 when Thomas Platter, a Swiss visitor to London wrote:

> After dinner on the 21st September, at about two o'clock, I went with my companions over the water, and in the strewn roof-house saw the tragedy of the first Emperor Julius with at least fifteen characters very well acted . . .

There is other evidence that this is the year of the play's first production, and so we may see it as coming at the height of Shakespeare's powers and at the very time when the success of his company was crowned by the opening of the new and splendid Globe. The play, as we know from writers of the time, had an immediate and lasting success and attracted the envy and imitation of other playwrights. Modern editions are listed in Part 5, Suggestions for further reading (p.91).

Part 2

Summaries
of JULIUS CAESAR

A general summary

The great Roman general, Julius Caesar, has become master of Rome
and some fear that he will become king. A group of young men led by
Cassius plan to prevent this by assassinating him. They gain the support
of Brutus, a close friend of Caesar but a passionate republican. Brutus
becomes the leader of the conspirators, who escort Caesar to a meeting
of the Senate and there stab him to death. At Caesar's funeral Antony,
who has been given Brutus's generous permission to speak in praise of
Caesar, rouses the people against the conspirators who are forced to
escape from Rome.

Civil war breaks out between the supporters of Brutus and Cassius,
on the one hand, and the followers of Antony and Caesar's nephew,
Octavius, on the other.

Despite Cassius's warnings and the appearance of Caesar's ghost,
Brutus resolves to fight his enemies at Philippi. The battle goes badly
for Cassius and he commits suicide. Brutus fights on but is defeated. As
night falls he also kills himself.

Detailed summaries

Act I: Historical introduction

The play begins with Caesar at the height of his power and glory. He
has extended the boundaries of Roman rule, defeated his old fellow
ruler Pompey in a savage civil war, and is now the real master of Rome
and her subject territories. In theory Rome is still legally a Republic
ruled by her aristocratic senate with the consent of the common people
who are represented by the Tribunes, but in fact Caesar is king in all
but name. He would like to be king in name also, but this could bring
his despotism into the open and also revive memories of the wicked
kings expelled from Rome, by Brutus's ancestor and others, when the
Republic was founded. Even though Caesar is not yet king there is
already deep opposition to his rule.

Act I Scene 1: The mob rebuked

(*A public scene followed by a private conference. Short. Morning on the streets of Rome.*)

A happy crowd of holidaying Romans of the common people surge onto the stage and are halted by Flavius and Marullus, the Tribunes, who scold them for not being at work. They ask the business of some of the people and are civilly answered by a carpenter, and cheekily by a cobbler who finally tells them that they 'make holiday to see Caesar, and to rejoice in his triumph'. This is public celebration, which Plutarch said 'offended many', to mark Caesar's final conquest of Pompey. Shakespeare, to speed up his plot, has conflated this with the Lupercal ceremonies, which occurred later, and timed them both on the day before the Ides of March (15th). Marullus now makes a fine speech reproving the people for rejoicing, reminding them of the greatness and popularity of Pompey, whose killing and whose killer they are now celebrating. Flavius seconds him and the crowd, ashamed and silent, creep away.

The Tribunes, left alone, plan to continue the work of driving the crowds off the streets and also to remove the decorations placed on statues of Caesar for the triumph. His ambitions must be curbed.

NOTES AND GLOSSARY:

Shakespeare is renowned for the power and variety of his opening scenes and this is a fine example. We know immediately that this is a public, political play and quickly feel not only the tension of the coming conflict between Caesar and those who resent his power, but also that this is a dangerous world in which great figures like Pompey can pass quickly from triumph to bloody death. The mob, first gay, then shame-faced in this scene, are to be one of the most important 'characters' in the play, and already we see how fickle they are, how easily turned and changed by the mood and rhetoric of the occasion. In the Tribunes we have our first taste of the public men of Rome. Their speech, at once austere and passionate, sets the tone for the play; and Marullus's recreation of the great days of Pompey does even more, for it creates Rome itself in the minds of the audience, the great buildings, the Tiber, the roaring crowds, the chariots, the garlands of honour and victory.

mechanical: workers, craftsmen
sign/Of your profession: tools, working clothes
in respect of: compared to
cobbler: a pun, he is a mender of shoes but the word also means a bad workman, a clumsy craftsman
directly: clearly

soles:	pun with 'souls'
naughty:	worthless
out with me:	angry
out:	with worn *out* shoes, pun with previous line's 'out with me'
mend you:	pun, improve your temper and mend your shoes
all . . . awl, . . . :	puns on the cobbler's piercing tool his awl, repeated in 'withal' two lines later
meddle:	pun, to interfere, also to have sex
recover:	pun, help them to get better, also re-cover
proper:	fine, good-looking
neat's:	cow's
triumph:	celebration of victory with a military procession
tribuaries:	conquered leaders who used to walk chained in the triumphal procession
senseless:	unfeeling
pass:	pass through
replication:	echo
attire:	clothes
cull out a holiday:	pick, or choose a free day; the word 'cull' is used for picking flowers and fits in with the next line: they pick the day and the flowers to honour Caesar
intermit:	withhold (a legal punishment)
till the lowest stream . . . :	until their tears fill up the riverbed from the lowest to the highest water mark
basest mettle:	pun, poor quality and hence inferior character. Flavius is saying 'Look, even these low characters feel the effect of our words.'
disrobe the images:	strip the statues (of Caesar) which had been decorated with wreaths
decked with ceremonies:	decorated with wreaths or crowns—according to Plutarch to encourage 'the common people to call him King'
Lupercal:	a great fertility feast held on 15 February. Shakespeare has combined this with Caesar's earlier triumph held some four months before
vulgar:	common people
thick:	crowding
These growing . . . fearfulness:	an image from Falconry; the wing feathers of the hunting hawks were pulled out or trimmed to control the height and distance they could fly, as the tribunes wish to control Caesar's political range
pitch:	height

Act I Scene 2: Lupercal. Cassius approaches Brutus

(*Public scene, private conference, public scene, private conference. Long. Later the same day on the same streets.*)

The mob crowds back on to the stage, and then divides to make way for a procession which comes in to the sound of drums and trumpets. Here is great Caesar himself with his wife Calphurnia, Brutus reserved and thoughtful with his wife Portia; Cicero, the eminent writer and Senator; Decius, courtier, flatterer and conspirator; Cassius, thin and restless, the master plotter; the fine figure of the young soldier, Mark Antony, stripped for the holy race of the Lupercalia; the bluff and cynical Casca; and others of the officials and nobility of Rome. Notice the Tribunes following, probably at a distance, to see where Caesar's ambitions will lead on this public occasion.

The first twenty-four lines show us the absolute mastery of Caesar. His every wish is anxiously met. When he speaks the music is stilled. His name is repeated again and again. And yet both incidents in the short passage show the human vulnerability of this demi-god: he has no child, so he orders Antony to touch Calphurnia in the sacred race; he is not divine but mortal, and as the warning of the soothsayer reminds him and us, he is in danger.

The trumpets sound again and all leave to see the 'holy chase' except for Brutus, and Cassius who has been watching Brutus closely. Though Brutus wants to be left alone, Cassius insists on talking to him and accuses him of being unfriendly. Brutus excuses himself by saying that he is 'at war' 'with himself' and that his inner troubles make him neglect his friends. If that is the case, says Cassius, he has something to tell him about himself: Cassius, like many others, wishes that in these bad times Brutus had a clearer idea of his own potential. Brutus fears that Cassius is trying to lead him into some danger, probably implying that Cassius is seeking, as indeed he is, to involve him in treason. Cassius replies passionately: he will show Brutus his own true self, he is not to be suspected by Brutus since he is no flatterer, gossiper, scandalmonger.

He is interrupted by the sound of trumpets and a distant shout, and Brutus, almost in spite of himself breaks out:

'What means this shouting? I do fear the people
Choose Caesar as their King!'

Cassius sees his advantage and exclaims:

'Ay, do you fear it?
Then I must think you would not have it so.'

Brutus admits it and then asks Cassius what it is he wants to say or to suggest. If it is something for the public good he will risk even death in such a cause.

With this encouragement Cassius launches into a long passionate and brilliant speech, only interrupted dramatically half-way through by another distant shout and trumpet blast which he uses for emphasis. Who is this Caesar? he asks: a mortal man subject to sickness and death like anyone else; in fact a feeble enough specimen. Yet now he is the *only* man who counts in Rome, a giant, a hero, a god. Everyone, even Brutus, is overshadowed; Rome is disgraced, reduced to one Roman. Once there was a Brutus who never would have allowed any man to be king in Rome.

The reserved and stoic Brutus is moved, but he answers in an ordered and reasoned way. He trusts Cassius as his friend. He has a good idea of what Cassius is proposing. He will tell him his own thoughts later. Until then let Cassius be satisfied with the assurance that he, Brutus, is not prepared to see things go the way they seem to be going.

He says this with some feeling for Cassius answers that he is pleased to have 'struck fire' from him.

Now Caesar and his retinue come back across the stage returning from the games. Caesar looks angry, and Cassius asks Brutus to get Casca to stay behind to tell them why. Caesar notices Cassius staring at him, and calling Antony to his side warns him against such thin, restless, thoughtful men, contrasting him with the good-humoured Antony.

As Caesar and his followers leave, Casca stays to tell in his rough cynical way how the crown was offered to Caesar three times by Antony but how, seeing the crowd disliked the idea, he refused it three times. How the crowd cheered him and how he fell down in an epileptic fit, and then, recovering, offered the people his life. And finally of how the Tribunes had been 'put to silence' for taking the decorations from Caesar's statues.

Casca is invited to dinner with Cassius, accepts and leaves. Brutus also agrees to see Cassius the day after and goes on his way. Cassius, left to himself, tells the audience that, if he were in Caesar's favour, as is Brutus, instead of being disliked by Caesar, he would never join the plot. He will further his work on Brutus by placing anonymous messages in Brutus's house, encouraging his republican pride, and hinting at Caesar's tyranny.

NOTES AND GLOSSARY:
In Cassius's encounter with Brutus the main line of action in the play is energetically begun. The contrast between these two men, so skilfully employed throughout the play, is well established: Cassius excitable, talkative, full of passion and self-justification, bombarding the quiet sober Brutus with reason and rhetoric until he gets his way.

In this scene also we see Caesar clearly. This is the portrait of a great man, but of a great man who believes in and encourages his own legend: 'for always I am Caesar'. The portrait is a brilliant synthesis of consistencies and inconsistencies of power, of heroic strength and human weakness, of shrewdness and silliness. Antony, who will carry Caesar's power into the second half of the play, is merely sketched here: Shakespeare does not need him yet. Casca is a short but vivid portrait of the blunt cynic who sneers at everything, possibly because he is unsure of or dissatisfied with himself as we guess in later scenes: good material for a conspirator, as Cassius sees.

The scene is brilliantly arranged and varied, full of changing interest and tension, full of changing voices, groupings and stage effects.

The *way* each character speaks, not just what he says, tells us much about him; and there is also a development of the imaginary world which is steadily being built up by the poetry of the play. Honour, courage, and greatness are further emphasised, but to these are added new images of generosity and comradeship which are central to the world of *Julius Caesar*, and which are even to be found powerfully active in Cassius's stories about Caesar: the friends swimming the raging river side-by-side, the great general, sick on campaign, asking for a drink from the hand of a comrade (Cassius himself is later to say: 'I cannot drink too much of Brutus love').

shake off:	are freed from
set on:	move forward
press:	crowd
ides of March:	15 March
soothsayer:	a person with prophetic powers, with second sight
throng:	crowd
order of the course:	progress of the race
gamesome:	light-hearted, fond of sports and games
quick spirit:	liveliness
as I was wont to have:	as I used to have
too stubborn and too strange a hand:	unfriendly cold behaviour
Be not deceived . . . myself:	his troubled looks only reflect his inner troubles
passions of some difference:	conflicting feelings
conceptions only proper to myself:	private thoughts
give some soil . . . to my behaviours:	make me behave badly
construe:	interpret
mistook your passion:	misinterpreted your feelings
By means . . . buried:	so that I have kept hidden
'Tis just:	exactly so
shadow:	reflection

best respect:	highest reputation
glass:	mirror
jealous on:	suspicious of
common laughter:	someone people make fun of (may be a mistake for laugher in which case it means someone who jokes with everyone)
or did use . . . protester:	or if it were my custom to swear friendship, with tavern oaths, to every new person wanting to know me
fawn on:	flatter, make up to
scandal:	speak ill of
profess myself:	promise friendship
rout:	mob
general:	public
speed me:	bring me success
favour:	appearance
as leif not be:	rather not exist
raw:	cold
chafing with:	raging against
accout'red:	dressed in armour
And stemming . . . controversy:	pushing it back with aggressive competitive feelings
Aeneas:	the Trojan hero supposed to have come to Italy after the fall of Troy and founded the Roman state
Anchises:	Aeneas's father
mark:	notice
His coward . . . fly:	his lips went pale—a military pun: to fly from one's colours means to abandon the battle flag, to run away
bend:	look, glance
his:	its
temper:	constitution, physique
get the start of:	surpass
bear the palm:	get the winner's prize
Colossus:	giant statue (as that of Apollo which is reputed to have stood over the entrance to Rhodes harbour)
stars:	fixed fate
sounded more:	more famous, literally 'spoken'
start a spirit:	(*i*) conjure up a ghost or supernatural power or (*ii*) excite a mind
meat:	food
since the great flood:	the Romans had the legend of a flood long ago which had drowned everyone except one good man and his wife

famed with:	famous for
Rome . . . room:	pronounced the same in Shakespeare's London
a Brutus:	the patriot ancestor of the Brutus of the play
nothing jealous:	not at all doubtful
What you . . aim:	what you want to make me do I have some idea of
meet:	suitable
chew upon this:	ruminate (think) about this
Train:	following, retinue
chidden:	scolded
ferret:	red-eyed like a ferret
crossed in conference:	opposed in debate
well given:	good-natured
Yet if . . . fear:	if I were the sort of man who would be afraid
hears:	listens to
sort:	way
sad:	serious
put it by:	pushed it to one side
marry:	truly (from the oath 'by (the Virgin) Mary')
Coronets:	small or plain crowns
fain:	gladly
the rabblement . . . hands:	the crowd cheered and clapped their rough hands
nightcaps:	scornful description of soft caps worn by the working people
swounded:	fainted
soft:	take it slowly
like:	probable
falling sickness:	epilepsy
use to do:	usually do to
pluck'd me ope his doublet:	opened his jacket collar (Caesar really wore Roman robes but the Elizabethans imagined and showed him dressed in their doublet and hose with a large 'Roman' cloak)
a man of any occupation:	a pun (*i*) one of the tradesmen in the crowd (*ii*) a man of initiative and action
Greek to me:	old saying 'I couldn't understand it' (in fact the real Casca seems to have known Greek!)
put to silence:	silenced, by being dismissed from office, banished or executed
promised forth:	have another appointment to go out
dine:	eat (usually at mid-day, 'sign' would be for the evening meal)
hold:	stays the same
quick mettle:	lively

tardy form:	appearance of stupidity or sullenness
rudeness:	rough manner
wit:	intelligence
disgest:	digest, appreciate
world:	the state of public affairs
mettle may be wrought:	character may be worked on, shaped (a pun on working metal into a tool or weapon, or frame chemically changing the nature of a metal by alchemy)
that it is disposed:	its natural characteristics
meet:	suitable, right
bear me hard:	dislikes me
in several hands:	in different handwritings
tending to the great opinion:	suggesting the high opinion
glanced at:	suggested
seat him sure:	put himself in a safe situation

Act I Scene 3: Storm and stress

(*Private conference. Short. Nightfall of the same day. The same streets.*)

A pause with empty stage. Thunder begins to rumble and grows in volume. A terrified Casca enters with drawn sword and meets Cicero, who is less moved by the fierce weather and by those fearful supernatural signs which Casca now describes vividly for us. Cicero goes off, and Cassius comes in, seemingly excited by the wild night. He tells Casca that he has been wandering round the streets tempting the 'cross blue lightning' to strike him. Casca says a man should beware of the anger of the gods, but Cassius answers that there are more monstrous things than these portents which are only symptoms of the evil state of affairs in Rome. There is a man in Rome more monstrous. Casca guesses it is Caesar. Without answering directly Cassius says that they are all slaves now. Casca, again more direct, speaks of the kingship of the Roman territories outside Italy which he has heard that the Senate are to offer to Caesar next day. If that happens, says Cassius, he himself will choose the freedom of death by suicide. Casca agrees, and Cassius says that if the Romans had any spirit left Caesar could never be a tyrant—but perhaps now Casca will betray him? Never, says Casca; rather he is ready to take part in any action to put things right. They shake hands and Cassius tells him that he has already gathered a band of noble Romans determined to undertake the dangerous and terrible work. They are to meet that night in Pompey's porch. At this point they are interrupted by the entrance of Cinna, who, as Cassius explains to Casca, is 'a friend'; that is, one of the conspirators. Cassius gives Cinna the task of placing the anonymous letters at Brutus's house, and Casca agrees that Brutus would be invaluable to them:

'O, he sits high in all the people's hearts;
And that which would appear offense in us,
His countenance, like richest alchemy,
Will chance to virtue and to worthiness.'

They will visit Brutus before morning, says Cassius, and make sure of his support.

NOTES AND GLOSSARY:
This scene shows Cassius as the centre of an active plot whose members are resolved on immediate action to prevent Caesar's speedy progress to the throne. All they lack is the support of Brutus, which they mean to get that very night. Our view of Cassius as an efficient inciter of conspiracy (seen earlier in his approach to Brutus) is now developed; we see him also as a determined and competent leader. Casca, already overawed by the strange night, is easily persuaded.

The storms and portents are exciting in themselves and they also give us a sense of the approach of terrible events. These warriors fighting in the sky, slaves with flaming hands, lions in the streets, are full of a sort of energy and grandeur which adds to the particular character of this play. Notice how different they are from the supernatural phenomena of other Shakespearean plays. Here is none of the death-horror of *Hamlet*, none of the evil of *Macbeth*.

sway of earth:	kingdom of earth
rived:	split apart
with:	to
saucy with:	insolent to
sensible of:	feeling
Against:	opposite
glazed:	stared
annoying:	harming
drawn/Upon a heap:	huddled together
ghastly:	pale
bird of night:	owl (a sign of bad luck)
conjointly meet:	happen together
portentous:	ominous
climate:	place, region
strange-disposèd:	disturbed
clean from the purpose:	quite wrongly
unbracèd:	with doublet open
thunder-stone:	thunderbolt, meteor

cross:	jagged, forked
the part of:	fitting for
astonish:	astound
want:	lack
And put on . . . wonder:	show fear and are amazed
from quality and kind:	(act) contrary to their nature and breed
old men:	senile men
calculate:	prophesy
ordinance:	usual order
performèd faculties:	inbred qualities
quality:	condition
spirits:	supernatural powers
prodigious:	like a supernatural threat
eruptions:	disturbances
thews:	muscles, sinews
Woe the while:	alas for these times
yoke:	wooden collar of slavery, meaning servitude
sufferance:	putting up with things
Therein:	in this power (of killing himself)
retentive to:	keep in
hinds:	pun (*i*) deer (*ii*) peasants or servants
my answer must be made:	I shall be accused (of treason)
indifferent:	unimportant
fleering:	sneering
Be factious:	form an action group or faction
by this:	by now
stay:	wait
Pompey's porch:	the doorway into Pompey's theatre
And the . . . element:	condition of the sky
favour:	appearance
close:	hidden
incorporate/To:	committed to
on't:	of it
praetor's chair:	official chair of a chief magistrate
Where Brutus may but find it:	where only Brutus will find it
old Brutus:	see Act I, Scene 2, line 159
Repair:	go
hie:	hurry
sits high:	has an important place
countenance:	pun (*i*) face (*ii*) approval
alchemy:	the old science which attempted to change less precious metals into gold
conceited:	conceived, understood

Act II Scene 1: Brutus chooses

(Private conference. Long. The same night to the following morning. Brutus's orchard.)

Late at night the troubled Brutus is walking in his garden. He calls his boy-servant Lucius to light a candle in his study. When the boy goes to obey him he talks to himself about Caesar: Caesar is ambitious and almost certain to become king; and, though so far he has been reasonable and humane, absolute power is almost certain to corrupt him and turn him to a tyrant; so he must die.

Lucius comes back with one of the anonymous letters (written, as we know, by Cassius), which he has found on the windowsill of Brutus's study. By the light of the meteors flying across the sky of that strange night Brutus reads the message urging him to save Rome, and promises to take action.

Lucius, who has been away to check the date, comes back to tell him that it is the Ides of March, and at that moment someone knocks at the gate. As Lucius goes to see who it is, Brutus, in a short but most revealing passage, speaks of the suspense and anxiety from which he has been suffering. Nothing less than the growing conviction that he himself must kill his friend can explain his words.

Lucius comes back to say that Cassius is outside with a group of others who cannot be recognised because of their pulled-down hats and muffled faces. He is sent to bring them in while Brutus muses about the difficulty of concealing a plot, unless one acts the hypocrite.

The conspirators enter and are introduced to Brutus by Cassius: they are Trebonius, Decius, Casca, Cinna, Metellus. Cassius then takes Brutus aside and speaks to him, doubtless explaining the plan to kill Caesar that very day in the Capitol. This may be symbolically echoed by Casca's speech about the sunrise. Brutus returns to the group and solemnly shakes hands with each man. He then rejects the idea of a secret oath as unworthy of honourable Romans whose simple word is enough. Cassius asks if they should try to recruit Cicero, but, in spite of general approval of the idea, Brutus will not have it:

'. . . For he [Cicero] will never follow anything
That other men begin.'

There is a fine irony in this, because Brutus, now just joined to the conspiracy, is steadily rejecting all the proposals made by the others and imposing his own will and ideas on the group.

Cassius says that Antony should die with Caesar, because he is a cunning planner and could put them all in danger. No, says Brutus, there must be no massacre; what they are doing is performing a sacred sacrifice to purge Rome of tyranny. Antony is only 'a limb of Caesar', harmless when Caesar is dead; and, besides, not to be taken seriously since he devotes his life 'to sports, to wildness, and much company.' Again Brutus has his way, to the future ruin of their fortunes.

The clock strikes three. Now Cassius asks what they should do if Caesar, grown superstitious these days, is frightened by the signs and portents and refuses to come to the Senate meeting at the Capitol. Decius answers confidently that he can get Caesar to come, by flattering him. They will all go to Caesar's house to fetch him. Caius Ligarius, a friend of Brutus who is out of favour with Caesar, is mentioned, and Brutus asks Mettellus to call at Caius's house and send him to Brutus so that he can be recruited.

The other conspirators leave Brutus. Lucius has fallen asleep, but now Brutus is joined by Portia, who gives us a vivid description of the troubled Brutus of the past weeks, and reproves him for not trusting her with whatever has been worrying him so much. She will prove to him that she can keep a secret. She has given herself a wound in her thigh to test her powers of silent endurance. Brutus is obviously deeply moved and promises to tell her everything.

They have been interrupted by another knocking at the gate, and, when Portia withdraws, Lucius brings in Caius Ligarius. He has risen from his sick-bed to come, but when he hears that Brutus has a plan of action he feels better and goes out with him towards Caesar's house, eager to take part in any action proposed by the noble Brutus.

NOTES AND GLOSSARY:
It will be necessary to return to this scene later when we come to discuss both Brutus and Cassius. For Brutus particularly it is a key scene, in some ways his most important, because in it we see him before the current of events has swept him some way from his own chosen ground. On our interpretation of and reaction to what he says here, particularly when he is alone, will depend our whole understanding of the play.

What sort of a man is this, choosing and planning to kill his friend for the common good? Do we accept or reject his reasons? Do we admire him or does he repel us? The wide differences of opinion concerning Shakespeare's Brutus reflect a real ambiguity and complexity in the play itself. Brutus himself may seem to speak with almost inhuman calmness of action and honour and sacrifice, but this is not the whole story, even for him: we know from Portia and from his own words what he is going through:

'Between the acting of a dreadful thing
And the first motion, all the interim is
Like a phantasma or a hideous dream.'

Such words reinforced by the deliberate setting of darkness, storm, disguise, fear and sickness show clearly that, however Brutus struggles for direct honour, what he is involved in is truly 'a dreadful thing'.

There are also arguments about Brutus's practical intelligence in leading the conspiracy. For instance his mistake about Antony is fatal. What we cannot doubt is his will and ability to take command. This, strengthened by the need and respect of the conspirators for him, enables him to take immediate and unquestioned command of things from the very first moments of his meeting with them. T. S. Dorsch is right, in his excellent introduction to the New Arden *Julius Caesar*, when he points out the irony of Cassius's fate. Cassius must be rid of Caesar because he cannot bear to be overshadowed by anyone. To be rid of Caesar he must turn to Brutus who immediately overshadows and overrules him.

Those who judge Brutus harshly would do well to remember that Shakespeare here gives us a man who has inspired the devotion of a beautiful, high-spirited and intelligent wife, and also of friends like Caius Ligarius, and servants like the boy Lucius.

Brutus is a complex portrait and all the more realistic for that.

The flexibility of time on the Elizabethan stage has been mentioned. This scene gives us an example of what has been called Shakespeare's 'double time'. It can be proved, on the one hand, that this is certainly the night after the Lupercal scene, yet listening to Brutus and Portia there is a strong impression that some considerable time has passed since Cassius came to Brutus about Caesar. 'Since Cassius *first* did whet me against Caesar/ I have not slept' (my italics)—this certainly sounds as if they have had several talks, and, if it does mean the day before, Brutus's grumble about losing one night's sleep is a little unheroic!

What Shakespeare is in fact doing is creating two co-existing time scales: first a sense of the rapid rushing on of events which makes the play more exciting; and, second, a sense of enough time passing for ideas and feelings to gradually develop in his characters so that we get a sense of psychological depth and probability. He does this in a number of plays: *Othello* contains the most startling example of all.

progress of the stars: the movement of the stars
. . . when? what . . .!: expressions of impatience
taper: candle
spurn at: rebel against, kick against
for the general: for public reasons
It is the bright day . . . adder: good weather brings out poisonous snakes, that is, good fortune and power bring out the dangerous things in men

craves:	demands
danger:	harm
Th'abuse . . . power:	rank is badly used when it separates power from compassion
swayed:	controlled (him)
But 'tis a common . . . ascend:	an extended image of climbing a ladder as a metaphor for the rise to political power
proof:	knowledge
lowliness:	humility
round:	rung, step
base degrees:	pun: lower steps, lower ranks
prevent:	we must stop the possibility of its happening
quarrel:	action against Caesar
take no colour:	find no justification
fashion it thus:	argue in this way
augmented:	with more power
extremities:	extremes
as his kind:	according to his nature
mischievous:	harmful
closet:	study
exhalations:	meteors
piece it out:	interpret it, expand the meaning
under . . . awe:	in awe of one man
thy full petition:	everything you ask
whet:	sharpen, work me up
motion:	impulse
phantasma:	hallucination
genius:	inner spirit
mortal instruments:	natural faculties
The nature of an insurrection:	a kind of revolution
brother:	brother-in-law (Cassius was married to Brutus's sister)
moe:	more
hats:	an anachronism—on the Elizabethan stage if a character pulled down his hat over his face he was 'unrecognisable'
discover:	recognise
favour:	appearance
path thy native semblance on:	walk in your true appearance
Erebus:	mythical dark region on the way to the land of the dead
upon your rest:	in disturbing your rest
What watchful . . . night:	what wakeful worries are preventing you from resting

fret:	mark with lines
growing on:	encroaching on
Weighing:	considering
high:	direct
face of men:	the sincere looks of the conspirators
sufferance:	suffering
time's abuse:	the corruption (political) of the times
betimes:	at once
So let . . . range on:	so let proud dictatorship hunt freely (like a falcon)
lottery:	by the chance whim of the tyrant
prick:	spur
secret Romans:	trustworthy in keeping a secret because Roman (noble)
palter:	play tricks of speech, equivocate
honesty:	honour
engaged:	committed, promised
swear:	swear in
cautelous:	crafty, deceitful
carrions:	literally dead bodies, that is, as good as dead
even:	steadfast
unsurpressive mettle:	unconquerable quality
or . . . or:	either . . . or
bastardy:	unfaithfulness, being untrue to Roman blood
no whit:	not at all
break with him:	tell him
of him:	in him
shrewd contriver:	skilful plotter
annoy:	harm
envy:	malice, hatred
spirit of Caesar:	(which Brutus sees as) tyranny
come by:	get to
gentle:	noble
This shall . . . envious:	to make it plain we act from political necessity, not personal malice
purgers:	cleansers—pun on cleaning, in the old system of medicine by bleeding or purging the patient
ingrafted:	firm-rooted
much he should:	surprising if he went so far
no fear:	nothing to be afraid of
Quite from . . . held once:	quite opposite to the strong views he once had
ceremonies:	omens
apparent:	clear
augurers:	priests who tried to tell the future by various magical means

o'ersway him: persuade him otherwise
That unicorns ... toils: ways of trapping wild animals
glasses: mirrors
holes: pits
toils: snares, nets
For I can ... bent: for I can work on his true character
uttermost: latest
bear Caesar hard: finds Caesar hard to put up with
rated: berated, rebuked
by him: to his house
fashion: work on
put on: show
bear it: behave
formal constancy: steady behaviour
Manet: (*Latin*) remains
figures: imaginings
ungently: rudely
across: folded—a conventional position for melancholy brooding
wafter: wave
withal: also
but an effect of humor: just a mood
his: its
condition: behaviour, disposition
know you: recognise you as
come by: get
physical: healthy
unbraced: unbuttoned
suck up the humors: breathe in the dampness—night air was thought to be unhealthy
vile contagion: evil infection
rheumy: cold and damp
unpurgèd: unpurified (by the light and heat of the sun)
sick offence: harmful sickness
place: as his wife
charm: entreat, conjure
incorporate: join
heavy: sad
had resort: visited
Is it expected: is there a law
in sort or limitation: within (legal) restrictions
suburbs: outside the centre
withal: also
Cato: famous for courage and honesty

counsels:	secrets
constancy:	reliability
engagements:	commitments
construe:	explain, interpret
All the . . . brows:	all that is written in the worried lines of his forehead
How?:	How are you?
vouchsafe:	accept
brave:	fine
kerchief:	cloth around the head worn by the sick
derived . . . loins:	sprang from a noble family
exorcist:	one who conjures up spirits
mortified:	sick
whole:	healthy
set on:	advance

Act II Scene 2: Caesar chooses

(Private conference then Public scene. Medium length. The same morning, just after the previous scene. At Caesar's house.)

The storm returns and now we are in Caesar's house. He comes in, in his dressing gown, and asks a servant to order the priests to make sacrifice and read the omens for the day: which they used to do by various means, including an inspection of the inner organs of birds and animals which had been sacrificed.

Calphurnia comes in full of terror at the portents, at her dreams, at the storm, and begs Caesar not to go out. At first he resists her, and also the ominous news of a sacrificed animal without a heart. It is only when his wife goes on her knees to him and begs him to stay that he relents and agrees to let Antony tell the senate that he is not well. Possibly he is glad to be persuaded.

At this crucial point Decius comes in to take him to the Senate House. Caesar asks him to tell the Senate he will not come, and now he rejects Calphurnia's excuse of sickness and tells Decius to tell them simply that he does not choose to come. Decius pleads for some reason lest he 'be laughed at'. No, says Caesar, it is enough for the Senate that he does not want to come; but he will tell his friend Decius the reason: Calphurnia is afraid, and has had a dream of Caesar's statue bleeding from many wounds and of the Romans bathing their hands in the blood.

Now Decius shows his skill as flatterer. The real meaning of the dream, he says, is that Caesar shall give life to all Rome. Caesar is pleased by this and Decius presses his advantage: the Senate are resolved to offer Caesar a crown that very day, he says, and if Caesar does not come they may change their minds. Also, he suggests, Caesar may be mocked if it becomes known that he is frightened by the dreams of his wife. He apologises for being so blunt, excusing himself as being concerned for Caesar.

Decius has prevailed, and Caesar is now fully resolved to go. In come the other conspirators except for Cassius (whom Caesar dislikes). Antony also enters. All are greeted warmly by Caesar who will share a cup of wine with them before they all set out for the Capitol. Brutus's last remark shows his grief in betraying his friend, but there is no hesitation despite the sorrow he feels.

NOTES AND GLOSSARY:

Here we see again the humanity and vulnerability of Caesar and also his overweening pride and conceit. As in the portrait of Brutus we get the complexity of personality influenced by action and power. On the whole our sympathies are swung rather to Caesar's side in this scene as the plot quickens towards his death. His warmth and hospitality to his killers at the end of the scene is clearly meant to be striking, and it sharpens Brutus's pain at what he must do.

Calphurnia's pleading with Caesar, effective in itself, also is in pleasing contrast and parallel to Portia's scene with Brutus, that balancing of scenes and characters which Shakespeare is always using and which is particularly symmetrical in this play.

nightgown:	dressing gown
present:	immediate
success:	whether or not the time is lucky
stood on ceremonies:	took notice of omens
watch:	night guard
yawned:	opened wide
right form of war:	correct battle formation
hurtled:	clashed
beyond all use:	utterly unusual
to:	meant for
Blaze forth:	announce (in fire)
Caesar . . . heart:	Caesar would be like a heartless (cowardly) animal
Your wisdom . . . confidence:	your good sense is destroyed by self-confidence
humor:	mood, whim
fetch:	escort
happy:	lucky, suitable
stays:	keeps
lusty:	healthy, strong
apply for:	counts as
press:	crowd

For tinctures ... cognisance: as medicines (or charms), honours, holy relics, marks of patronage or favour
a mock/Apt to be rendered: a sneering joke likely to be made
love/To your proceeding: concern for your career
liable: subject
robe: toga
That every like ... upon: That things are not the same as they seem (friendly), grieves the heart of Brutus

---

Act II Scenes 3 and 4: In the streets, warnings and fears

(*Private conference and Public scene. Both short. Just after the foregoing scene. The streets of Rome.*)

Now the whole movement of the play is towards the Senate House, towards the death of Caesar. Going to the Capitol we meet Artimodorus, a teacher of rhetoric who has discovered the plot. He has a paper warning Caesar, which he hopes to give to the dictator as he passes by. He goes off, or simply moves up stage, and Portia comes in with Lucius whom she is sending to the Capitol to bring news. She is confused and shaken by anxieties and fears. They meet the soothsayer who is also going to try to warn Caesar again. Lucius and the soothsayer go on. Portia goes home.

NOTES AND GLOSSARY:
Here we get a build-up of tension and impetus. Here also we see Portia shaking under the strain of the knowledge she begged for, feeling her weakness: 'I have a man's mind, but a woman's might.' Her own death is foreshadowed in this nervous crisis but Shakespeare makes her more determined than in the portrayal of her given by Plutarch. Here she says, 'Say I am merry', while Plutarch relates that the real Portia tried to persuade Brutus to come home by sending a report that she was dangerously ill.

bent: directed
look about you: beware
security ... conspiracy: overconfidence exposes you to plots
lover: friend
suitor: one presenting a petition
Out of the teeth of emulation: out of the danger of malicious envy
contrive: plot, conspire
constancy: fortitude, resolution
might: strength
keep counsel: keep a secret

take good note: notice carefully
bustling rumor like a fray: confused sound like a battle
Sooth: truly
chance: happen
praetors: Roman judges
void: empty
merry: cheerful

Act III Scene 1: The death of Caesar

(*Public scene. Long. Just after the foregoing scene. The street outside the Capitol and the interior of the Senate House.*)

The trumpets sound again, and once more, surrounded by nobles including the conspirators (who have now been joined by Cassius), Caesar enters and makes his way through the crowd. Again he exchanges words with the soothsayer who tries to warn him for the last time. Artimedorus pleads with him to read his letter as something to do with his own personal good, but Caesar puts it off: 'What touches us ourself shall be last served.' Artimedorus tries to insist but is pushed aside, and the nobles enter the Senate House. Here before the meeting begins there are some nervous minutes while the conspirators wonder what Popilius knows, and if he is going to betray them to Caesar. Cassius seems badly shaken but is steadied by Brutus while the danger passes.

Now the murder plan begins to develop. Antony is taken away on some invented business by Trebonius. As Caesar declares the session begun, Metellus moves forward, supposedly to plead for his banished brother, but really to get close to his victim. Even before he can finish his petition Caesar speaks with measured and terrible pride refusing his request. Metellus turns, pleading for seconders. Brutus joins him, kissing Caesar's hand, immediately followed by Cassius who kneels at his feet. Again Caesar refuses in terms of unshakable pride. Cinna and Decius press forward, adding their voices, and Caesar is surrounded. Casca comes behind him and with the cry: 'Speak hands for me!' strikes the first blow.

Then they are all on Caesar, stabbing and hacking. At first he keeps his feet, tries to fight them off, but overcome by wounds and by the sight of his beloved Brutus among his attackers, he speaks his last reproach, covers his face, and falls dead at the foot of the statue of his old friend, enemy, and victim Pompey.

Shouts and screams. The Senators break and run. While other excited voices cry out for liberty, Brutus tries to calm the terrified people but they scatter away leaving just one old man too weak to escape, Publius. Brutus ignores the fears of a counter-attack by Caesar's friends, and concentrates on reassuring Publius that no harm is meant to anyone now that Caesar is dead. The old man staggers away leaving the group of conspirators round the body. Trebonius rejoins them with the news that Antony has 'fled to his house amazed' and that the city is in the grip of panic and confusion.

The young men, shaken and excited by what they have done and by fears and hopes of what may follow, try to come to terms with the situation. Brutus looking at his dead friend realises that they too may die, so what particular matter when? Casca answers that death itself may save a man from the fear of death. We remember the words of Caesar rejecting such fear:

'Cowards die many times before their deaths;
The valiant never taste of death but once.'

But Brutus did not hear the dead man speak these words and is not conscious of the irony of his hope that they have saved Caesar from years of fear. Brutus struggles to make the occasion solemn and significant. The idea of a royal sacrifice returns to him and he leads the others in bathing their hands in Caesar's blood. Cassius too is moved by the greatness of their deed and wonders how often in following ages the deed will be acted out again in the theatres of the future.

Now, their spirits calmed and raised, they are ready to go out and face Rome.

And, at this exact moment, a servant of Antony comes in, throws himself at their feet and begs that Antony himself may come to have explained to him how Caesar has deserved to die at the hands of the noble Brutus. Brutus is sure he can satisfy Antony and promises him safety. The servant runs to fetch his master, while Cassius mutters his doubts.

Antony must have been close by, for he enters almost immediately.

He ignores the welcome of Brutus. He ignores them all, and goes over to the body of his friend and leader and speaks a brief but ringing farewell. Then he turns to the assassins and tells them quietly that he is ready to die too. Brutus assures him passionately that no harm is meant to him, that what has been done was for the common good, that they want him as their friend; and the worried Cassius adds that, if Antony comes in with them, he will be given power in the new political arrangements.

Again Brutus promises that when the public panic has been stilled he can and will explain things to Antony's satisfaction, and now Antony moves through the group shaking each bloody hand, only to turn away in grief to speak again to the dead Caesar, praising him and asking his forgiveness for shaking hands with his killers.

Cassius, increasingly worried, asks Antony bluntly, can they count on him as a friend, and he answers that they can indeed, if they can satisfy him that they have done the right thing (but he knows in his heart that they cannot so satisfy him). Again Brutus expresses the calm certainty that he can convince Antony.

Antony says that is all he requires, except for permission to speak at Caesar's funeral. Brutus agrees readily, but is taken aside by Cassius who is afraid that Antony will rouse the people. No, says Brutus calmly: he, Brutus, will speak to the people first and also explain that Antony has their permission to deliver the funeral oration. Cassius is unhappy, but the authority of Brutus again prevails. So Antony is given charge of the body by Brutus and also permission to speak at the funeral, provided that in praising Caesar he does not blame the conspirators. Antony agrees and they leave him alone with the body.

Once alone, Antony's true feelings burst out in a great speech of grief and rage, foretelling revenge, death, and civil war. As he finishes there comes in a messenger from Caesar's grand-nephew and heir, Octavius, who is expected in Rome. Antony tells the messenger to come with him to the funeral to see how things turn out, and then to take word back to Octavius.

Together they carry the body out.

NOTES AND GLOSSARY:
This long exciting scene is brilliantly handled by Shakespeare. There are two changes of direction in the action which are closely linked: the first is, of course, the murder itself; the second, which critics have rightly called the hinge of the play, is the entry of Antony's servant. This trembling figure announces the counter-stroke, the reaction against the main action of the play. Antony, kept deliberately in the background so far, now emerges as the subtle and powerful champion of the dead Caesar, the doom of the men who have killed 'the foremost man of all this world'. This, as Granville-Barker* says, is how Shakespeare immediately renews the tension of the play which might otherwise have loosened after Caesar's death.

Again in this scene we see the confirmation and development of Caesar's arrogance and humanity, both of which lead him to his death. Again we see the nervous but shrewd Cassius overruled by a Brutus courageous, idealistic, generous, and fatally ignorant of real men, power, and politics.

*Harley Granville-Barker (1877–1946) whose theatrical productions of Shakespeare helped to restore knowledge of how the plays were meant to work. He said that they must always be most alive—even if roughly and rudely alive—in the theatre. His *Prefaces to Shakespeare* are very valuable, largely because of his vivid theatrical understanding and imagination.

The excitement of the second part of the scene, between Antony and the conspirators, is totally different from that of the first part, but in no way inferior. Antony is a gambler and seems to relish the risks he takes as he works his way, without one real lie, to the position from which he can strike down the killers of his friend and chief. He knows from the first, as his servant's message tells us, exactly where the weakness of the conspirators lies: in the generous, honourable, total self-confidence of Brutus, who must believe that if he, Brutus, has found an action right and necessary, no man on earth will be able to quarrel with his reasons. Reasons do not matter to Antony except to play Brutus along. All that matters to Antony is that Caesar has been killed and must be revenged.

One particularly fine touch is his shaking of the killers' hands. There is an effective echo of Brutus's shaking hands with each conspirator in II, 1.

The news of Octavius's approach sharpens the feelings of forces building up against Brutus, Cassius and the rest, who have *no real plan* of what to do after Caesar's death.

schedule:	paper, document
touches:	concerns
Sirrah, give place:	move out of the way, fellow
makes to:	moves towards
prevention:	being prevented
turn back:	come back alive
constant:	resolute, steady
change:	change expression
presently prefer:	present straight away
addressed:	prepared
puissant:	powerful
couchings . . . courtesies:	bowing down, crouching for
And turn . . . children:	and change established laws and customs into children's game
fond:	stupid
rebel blood:	uncontrolled emotions
quality:	(of firmness)
base spaniel fawning:	low cringing, obsequiousness, like a dog seeking favour
repealing:	recalling from banishment
freedom of repeal:	the granting of a return from banishment
I could . . . nerve me:	I could be persuaded to change my mind if I were the same sort of person as you, the sort of person who would ask others to change their minds, then their pleas might make me change mine

resting:	changeless
fellow:	equal
unnumb'red:	countless
apprehensive:	capable of feeling and thought
rank:	place
constant:	resolved
Wilt thou lift up Olympus?:	will you try to do the impossible? (Olympus was a great mountain in Greece, supposedly the home of the gods)
bootless:	uselessly, in vain
Et tu, Brutè?:	(*Latin*) And you, also, Brutus?
common pulpits:	the rostra in the forum from which the Roman public was addressed, but Shakespeare may also be referring to open air pulpits around London
enfranchisement:	the full rights of a Roman citizen
ambition's debt is paid:	Caesar's ambition has been rewarded as it should be (by death)
mutiny:	tumult
talk not of standing:	do not consider making an organised resistance
abide:	take the consequences of
As it were doomsday:	as if it were the day of judgement
And drawing . . . upon:	and extending the span of life that men set such value on
sport:	pretence, play-acting, entertainment
basis:	the stand of the statue
knot:	closely united group
grace:	do honour to
Soft:	wait
honest:	honourable
resolved:	told
thorough:	through
untrod state:	unknown condition of affairs
so:	if it
presently:	immediately
well to friend:	as a good friend
and my misgiving . . . purpose:	and my doubts always turn out to be uncomfortably accurate
to let blood:	a medical term meaning that someone had blood extracted from them for their health
rank:	full of disease, this was often supposed to be cured by letting blood
bear me hard:	hate me, have anything serious against me
purpled:	stained with blood
reek and smoke:	smell and steam

live: even if I should live
apt: ready, prepared
mean: means, way
pitiful: full of pity, merciful
leaden: soft, blunt
temper: quality
voice: vote
dignities: positions of power
deliver: explain
credit: honour, reputation
conceit: imagine
dearer: more deeply
corse: body, corpse
close: agree, make friends with
bayed: cornered, brought to bay like hunted deer
hart: pun on (*i*) heart, and (*ii*) a male deer
Signed in thy spoil: stained with your murder (blood)
Lethe: in classical mythology, a river divided the land of the living from the land of the dead. Here the dead drank and the water brought them forgetfulness of their previous life. The river of death in this case is the actual blood of Caesar, flowing from his body
stroken: stricken down
modesty: moderation
pricked in number of our friends: marked down (on a wax tablet)
on: go on with our plans
good regard: sound reasons
produce: show forth
order: ceremony
protest: proclaim
advantage: do good to
wrong: harm
fall: happen
tide of times: the changing currents of history
cumber: weigh down
in use: common, customary
custom of fell deeds: being used to fatal acts
ranging: hunting
Atè: the Greek goddess of quarrelling and revenge
confines: borders, regions
let slip: unleash, unloose
carrion: putrefying
big: swollen up with sorrow
passion: intense feeling

post:	literally, to ride fast on relays of horses, also simply used to hurry
Rome:	a pun on the Elizabethan pronunciation of the word as Room
try:	discover
cruel issue:	deed resulting from the cruelty

Act III Scene 2: The funeral of Caesar

(*Public scene. Long. Later the same day. The Forum.*)

A large crowd follows Brutus and Cassius as they come to the Forum to explain to the people of Rome why Caesar had to die. Some follow Cassius away to hear his speech, while some stay to hear Brutus who goes up into a pulpit, or speaker's rostrum, to address them.

Brutus quietens them, and asks them to pay close attention and to believe what he is going to tell them. He speaks of his own love for Caesar, but his greater love for Rome. Caesar's ambition, despite his noble qualities, would have made slaves of all of them, and so he had to die. His death could only offend those who wanted to be slaves and traitors. The crowd approve Brutus, and he goes on to promise justice and an open public record of what has happened.

At this moment Caesar's body, in a coffin draped with his blood-stained mantle, is carried in and placed below the pulpit. Antony walks behind the body, sad and apparently subdued.

Brutus welcomes him, says he will share the new freedom. As his final word he promises to kill himself if ever Rome requires his death.

The crowd are cheering Brutus. They want him for king! They will take him to his house in triumph! But, with a final gesture of suicidal generosity and stupidity, he orders them all to stay to hear Antony's funeral speech of praise. They obey, and he goes off alone.

Now the crowd turn to Antony, but in no friendly spirit. They are Brutus's men and he had better not speak ill of Brutus. Caesar was a tyrant who deserved his death. Antony meekly thanks them in the name of Brutus and goes up into the pulpit. After two attempts to get silence he begins to speak.

They need not be afraid that he will praise Caesar. Men usually remember the faults of the dead, not their virtues. 'So let it be with Caesar'. Brutus has told them Caesar was ambitious: *if* so, Caesar has paid for his fault. Antony has the permission of the noble Brutus and the other honorable conspirators to speak about the Caesar he knew:

'He was my friend, faithful and just to me;
But Brutus says he was ambitious,
And Brutus is an honourable man.'

In a half-puzzled way he begins to examine this idea of an ambitious Caesar. He was generous with the spoils of victory, he cared for the sufferings of the poor, he humbly refused the crown offered to him: *'Was this ambition?'*

The crowd are now growing confused and troubled, and Antony himself acts the part of a disturbed man protesting that he is not trying to prove Brutus and the others wrong, but he has to say what he knows. His feelings seem to take over as he asks, where has their love of Caesar gone to? He turns aside choked by emotion, giving the people time to talk over the things he has said, and to react to his grief. Already he has brought them a long way from their cheering of Brutus.

When he begins to talk again he has their full attention. He speaks of the pitiful change between Caesar's greatness and his death. But he will not, he says, wrong Cassius and Brutus by rousing the people to rebellion. Let Caesar suffer, let Antony suffer, let the people suffer, rather than the conspirators. Then, with fine effect he waves a document at them: Caesar's will! He cannot read it to them, but if he did they would worship the dead man for the riches he has left them.

Naturally the crowd roars for the will. Antony, pretending to be frightened by what he has done, says, no, he cannot read it, for if he told them their luck they would be enraged. They cry out the louder, and as he protests that he must not wrong the 'honourable men/ Whose daggers have stabbed Caesar . . .' they begin to cry out against Brutus and the others calling them traitors, villains, and murderers.

Now Antony has the crowd in his hand but he is going to make quite sure that when he lets them loose against his enemies they will be roused to fever-pitch. Well, he says, if they will force him to read the will let him first show them Caesar, the man who made it. He comes down and they form a wide ring around the hearse.

Antony lifts the bloody mantle of Caesar and shows it to them: the cloak of the great hero of Rome riddled by the blades of his killers, soaked in blood. He shows them the wounds made by Cassius, by Casca; and, worst and most deadly of all, by Brutus, Caesar's dearest friend: the killer-wound under which Caesar fell. And no longer concealing his real feelings Antony cries out:

'Oh what a fall was that, my countrymen!
Then I, and you, and all of us fell down,
Whilst bloody treason flourished over us.'

The crowd are weeping, will they weep at a mere cloak? He will show them something worth their tears, and he uncovers the body of Caesar.

Now they are shouting and screaming. They mill around, swearing revenge; they will kill all the traitors. But Antony will not yet let them go, he calls them back and works on them again, suggesting that the killers had private grudges against Caesar. Protesting that he has merely told them the truth in his own straightforward way, saying that if he were Brutus, now, instead of blunt simple Antony, he could rouse the very stones of Rome to mutiny.

They yell their agreement and again surge away, but again he calls them back. They have not yet heard the will! It is a mark of Antony's complete power over them that he has to remind them of this matter which concerns them so deeply. Now he tells them that Caesar has left each citizen a sum of money and all his private pleasure-grounds for public parks. 'Here was a Caesar! When comes such another?'

'Never, Never!' they yell and now at length he lets them loose to rage through Rome in search of the killers, tearing the place apart for fuel to burn Caesar's body on a funeral pyre—the pyre from which they will take fire to burn also the houses of Caesar's enemies.

Antony stands alone, well satisfied to let them do the work he has set them.

To him comes another messenger to tell him that Octavius is in Rome, at Caesar's house with Lepidus a friend and ally, and that Brutus and Cassius are fled from the city.

Antony goes to join Caesar's nephew and to take up power.

NOTES AND GLOSSARY:
This scene, the second half of the great double climax of the play, is almost entirely made up of the short speech of Brutus and the long speech of Antony. The speeches are often contrasted and it has been said that Brutus's speech appeals to reason and Antony's to emotion, but that is neither a useful nor an accurate way of contrasting the speakers and their words. Brutus's great appeal is not to reason, but to the spirit of dignity and liberty in his hearers—that is, to those feelings which mean most to the speaker himself. His style of speech is clean, balanced and classical. His argument is built up in clear strong lines like those of a Greek temple. There is a *presentation* of facts and feelings but no real *change* or *growth* of tone and theme.

Antony, on the other hand, moves from mood to mood, from style to style, and from argument to emotion, as his purpose and his progress in winning over the mob direct the tactics of his speech. Reason, feeling and rhetoric—he uses them all. He plays his own tunes on the crowd; pity, regret, love, grief, terror, horror, greed, hatred, fear—they respond to his words as he wills. And they are not alone; for few people seeing the play for the first time, and, up to this point, sympathetic to Brutus, can have escaped being shaken or even won-over by this magnificent oratory. Surely, we think, as we listen or read, Antony is right and Brutus and the rest are killers and traitors. But if we pay close attention to Shakespeare we may not be so sure. There is something ruthless and reckless about Antony. His words when he is left alone are terrible in their calm indifference to the horrors of civil disorder:

'Now let it work: Mischief thou art afoot
Take thou what course thou wilt.'

Here and in the next scene we see the mob at their worst. They are truly a blind foolish force which offers the crown to a man who has killed his ambitious friend for wanting to be king, and which a short time later is howling for the blood of that same man.

The funeral scene shows the counterstroke against the conspirators completed. They have been outwitted, defeated and driven ignominiously from Rome. For the next two scenes they vanish in eclipse.

Satisfied:	have things explained to us
part the numbers:	split up the people into different groups
severally:	separately
lovers:	close friends
Censure:	judge
senses:	powers of judgement
bondman:	slave
rude:	uncivilised
shall do:	be given the power to do if Brutus also becomes a tyrant
The question of his death is enrolled in the Capitol:	the facts of his death have been recorded publicly
extenuated:	depreciated
enforced:	stressed, exaggerated
a place in the commonwealth:	full Roman citizenship
lover:	dear friend
qualities:	characteristics
do grace:	give honour to
tending:	concerning
public chair:	rostrum, pulpit
beholding:	grateful
answered:	paid for
general coffers:	public treasury
dear abide it:	pay dearly for it
none so poor:	not even the poor
closet:	study
commons:	ordinary people, plebians
napkins:	handkerchiefs
issue:	children
meet:	suitable
stay:	wait

o'ershot myself:	gone too far
far:	further
mantle:	cloak or toga
Nervii:	a Gaulish tribe conquered by Caesar
envious:	malicious
as:	as though
to be resolved:	to make sure
unkindly:	(pun) (*i*) savagely (*ii*) unnaturally
angel:	someone admired and loved as perfectly good
most unkindest:	(double superlative), most unkind, most unnatural
base:	stand, pedestal
flourished:	triumphed, waved its arms or weapons
dint:	blow, force
vesture:	clothes
marred:	spoilt
with:	by
About:	move off
private griefs:	personal grievances
public:	permission to speak in public
writ:	a written script of a speech
action:	effective gestures
utterance:	power of speaking well
right on:	directly
ruffle up:	stir up
several:	separate
royal:	princely
walks:	parks
orchards:	gardens
common pleasures:	public parks or playing fields
forms, windows:	benches and wooden shutters
work:	(pun) to work itself out or to ferment
will I straight:	I will go directly
upon a wish:	as I wanted
Are rid:	have ridden
belike:	it is likely
notice:	news

Act III Scene 3: Mob murder

In case we have missed the less pleasant aspects of mob rule in the previous scene, Shakespeare shows us the crowd on the rampage. They find an unfortunate poet called Cinna on the street, bully him, beat him up and finally take him away to kill him because he has the wrong name.

NOTES AND GLOSSARY:
Here clearly we see Shakespeare's horror of the savagery which comes with civil riot and war, when men are reduced so often to the lowest common denominator. Part of the surrealistic nightmarish quality of the scene lies in the fact that it is almost comic. Shakespeare knew that the grotesque is never far from violence and terror.

Notice also the hulking inefficiency of the mob. They were let loose by Antony to kill conspirators, and, instead, they kill innocent men while Caesar's murderers escape.

tonight:	last night
fantasy:	imagination
forth:	out of
directly:	immediately
bear me a bang:	get a blow from me
turn him going:	finish him off

Act IV Scene 1: The Triumvirate formed

(*Private conference. Short. Soon Afterwards. A private house (Caesar's ?).*)

Rome is now in the hands of Antony, Octavius and Lepidus. We find them playing deadly power politics with the lives of friends and relations. Antony then sends off Lepidus to get Caesar's will so that they can falsify the accounts and get more money for themselves.

When he has gone Antony begins to attack the character of Lepidus, saying that he is a nobody, and asking if he is fit to share the Roman Empire with them. Octavius protests that Antony has already treated him as an equal by giving him a say in the lists of those to be condemned; but Antony, claiming the privilege of age and experience, explains that they are using Lepidus to do their dirty work and to take the blame for their unpopular decisions and that later they will force him into unrewarded retirement.

Again Octavius protests, saying that Lepidus is a good soldier, but again Antony insists that Lepidus is a mere war-horse to be ridden hard and taught to obey: a mere follower and imitator.

Then Antony speaks of the great task that confronts them: Brutus and Cassius are raising armies against them and they must use all their skill and energy to fight back against open and hidden enemies. Octavius agrees.

NOTES AND GLOSSARY:
After the central climax of any play the dramatist is faced with an inevitable falling off of excitement and tension. He must keep the interest of the audience by introducing new elements in character and

conflict. Shakespeare does this, here, by bringing in Octavius and Lepidus, hinting at the tensions within the triumvirate, and by emphasising the dangers of the new politics and the approach of open civil war.

Antony, ruthless and hypocritical, is at his worst; and this, as has been often pointed out, will help those of the audience who may have been turned against Brutus to move back into sympathy with him, and so be in a better position to share the tragic experience of the last two acts. There is a sharp contrast between the Brutus who insisted that only Caesar must die and the Triumvirs who so easily toss away the lives of their own relations and friends.

At the same time we must remember that this darkening political scene is the direct consequence of Brutus's idealistic choice and action. After betrayal, to use a phrase of Eugene Watters, 'neither blood nor bone are innocent any longer.'

In Shakespeare's adaptation of Plutarch we see, here, the most striking use of compression in the play. Watching or reading Shakespeare you would almost think that this was the evening of the funeral day (see III, 2, lines 265-9), while from Plutarch we learn of a long confused period of antagonism and manoeuvering before the Triumvirate was formed. Shakespeare simply cuts out, or just hints at, periods or incidents which do not add to the direct thrust of the play.

pricked:	marked off on a list
cut off some charge:	cut down expenditure by falsifying the accounts of the amount Caesar had left
Or . . . or:	either or
slight unmeritable:	unimportant and undeserving
meet:	suitable
threefold world:	the Roman empire was divided into the areas of Asia, Europe and Africa
voice:	vote, say
proscription:	condemnation
To ease . . . loads:	to relieve ourselves of the weight of blame of various things we have done
business:	work
turn him off:	dismiss him
empty:	unburdened
in commons:	literally, on the public land where anyone was allowed to graze their cattle
appoint him store:	allocate him a supply
wind:	steer or turn
corporal:	physical
taste:	extent
so:	like that

barren-spirited: uninventive, unoriginal

On objects . . . imitations: rejected things, scraps and styles set by other people

staled: used up, made ordinary

begin: are the beginning of (Antony is saying that what other people have finished with Lepidus considers original and in fashion)

property: an instrument or tool

levying powers: raising armed forces

straight make head: immediately gather forces

our best friends made: form our closest alliances

stretched: extended to fullest advantage

presently: immediately

How covert . . . answered: how secret plots may be discovered and open dangers met most efficiently

at the stake: at risk (the image is taken from the baiting of savage animals who were tied to a post set in the ground and attacked by dogs trained for this 'sport')

bayed about: surrounded by (the metaphor is continued from the previous line—it means the dogs barking around the tied animal)

mischiefs: plots to damage us

Act IV Scenes 2 and 3: The quarrel and the ghost

(*Public scene and then Private conference. Short and then long. Evening and all night. Some time later at Brutus's camp at Sardis, and in his tent.*)

These scenes are put together as they are continuous. At the end of Scene 2 in the Elizabethan theatre, the 'armies' would go off the outer stage or withdraw to the edges of it, while Brutus and Cassius went into the tent, which was almost certainly represented by the inner stage whose doors or curtains would be opened to allow the audience to follow the action.

Brutus at his camp meets officers from his army and from that of Cassius. It is clear that Lucilius, one of Brutus's officers, has been to the army of Cassius and has come back with Pindarus and Titinius who bring Cassius's greeting and news of his approach. It is obvious from Brutus's words to them that there is trouble between the two leaders of the republican armies, and this is confirmed when Brutus takes Lucilius aside to ask him how he was received by Cassius and to express his conviction that Cassius's friendship is cooling.

When Cassius arrives he immediately accuses Brutus of wronging him. He is full of rage and grief and resentment. Brutus points out coolly that they must not damage the morale of their troops by squabbling in front of them, and invites him into his tent to discuss things in private. They go in, and Scene 3 follows immediately.

Cassius repeats his accusation: Brutus has condemned a friend of his for accepting bribes, in spite of Cassius's pleas for the guilty man. Cassius was wrong to support such a man, says Brutus. This is no time for fussing about such things, says Cassius, but Brutus presses home his attack by saying that Cassius is known himself for taking bribes and selling places of power.

Anyone but Brutus would die for saying that, cries the furious Cassius.

Anyone but Cassius would have been punished for such corruption, answers Brutus and continues his harsh reproofs despite Cassius's angry protests and threats.

When Cassius claims that he is the older and better soldier Brutus scorns him, and then defies him when he threatens violence. Brutus is not going to be bullied, he laughs at threats and temper.

Poor Cassius, reduced almost to speechlessness by Brutus's firmness and cold scorn, begins to hedge and bluster.

More threats from Cassius and more scornful insults from Brutus and then Brutus's own grievances against Cassius pour out in an indignant speech. Brutus needed money and Cassius had it. Brutus cannot debase himself by raising cash and Cassius refused to send him some to pay his army. Had he money and Cassius needed it he would never refuse it to a friend.

Cassius denies that he refused it, and says it was all a mistake. Then he goes on to complain that Brutus has broken his heart:

'A friend should bear his friend's infirmities;
But Brutus makes mine greater than they are.'

Brutus continues to be hard and severe until Cassius shows just how deeply he has been hurt by his friend's anger and scorn. He offers Brutus his dagger, telling him to cut out his heart: Brutus thinks that he refused him gold—let him take his heart instead.

Now, half laughing, Brutus tells him to put away his dagger. He cannot keep up his disapproval and anger.

Cassius, still hurt, asks if his rage and grief are only to be a joke to his friend, and Brutus with his first show of real emotional generosity in the scene, admits that he was bad-tempered too.

For Cassius, longing for reconciliation, this is enough. He holds out his hand which Brutus takes with words of genuine warmth.

Then while Brutus is being patronising about Cassius's temper (in what he probably thinks is a friendly way) a poet comes in to make peace between the generals, who send him about his business.

Lucilius and Titinius are despatched to order the night camp and to fetch Messala for a staff conference. Meanwhile Lucius will bring a bowl of wine to the commanders.

While they are alone Brutus explains to Cassius that his own anger was because he is 'sick of many griefs'. Cassius gently chides him for forgetting his stoic principles but Brutus says quietly:

'No man bears sorrow better. Portia is dead.'

He goes on to explain that Portia, driven to distraction by her fears for him, 'swallowed fire' and died. Cassius exclaims in grief; but, as Lucius comes in with the wine, Brutus asks him not to speak about her any more.

They drink together to their friendship.

The officers come in, and the news of the enemy army and of the political executions in Rome is discussed. After the death of Cicero is mentioned, we come to a strange passage in which Messala, who has heard of Portia's death, is persuaded to tell of it by Brutus, who says he has had no news of her. Having made Messala tell him, Brutus takes the news with the utmost stoicism. (This passage, and the discussion of Portia's death with Cassius, will be considered in the notes to this scene).

Now a plan of action against Antony and Octavius is discussed; and, once more, Brutus rejects Cassius's sound advice. It is the Antony business all over again, and, after the emotional beating that Cassius has taken in the quarrel, he is, if anything, even less able to stand against Brutus's wrongheaded certainty of being in the right. Brutus has his way: they will move down to Philippi the following day and fight their enemies there.

It is time to take a short rest. Friendly good-nights are said. Cassius and the other officers go out. Varro and Claudius are to sleep as guards in Brutus's tent. Brutus puts on his dressing-gown, looks for the book he is reading, and asks the faithful Lucius to sing him a song to the lute.

As he sings the guards nod off, and Lucius himself falls asleep with his lute in his lap. Brutus gently takes the instrument from the drowsy boy and turns to his book.

The candle flame dwindles. Something or someone moves forward out of the shadows of the tent and suddenly Brutus is stricken with fear. Who is it? It looks like Caesar.

Speak to me what thou art!
Thy evil spirit, Brutus.

The ghost tells him it will see him again at Philippi, and, as he rouses his courage and moves towards it, it vanishes. The guards cry out in their sleep and the boy wakes complaining that his lute is out of tune. None of them has seen anything, so Brutus pulls himself together, realises that it is nearly morning, and sends a message to Cassius to prepare to march.

NOTES AND GLOSSARY:
In these scenes Shakespeare re-establishes our intimacy with Brutus and Cassius while at the same time pressing on the action towards the final catastrophe. Taken together the two scenes form the longest sequence of action in the play, a sequence which balances the long scene in Brutus's orchard in Act II, Scene 1. Like that earlier scene, it is a private heartsearching before public action, but the famous and brilliant quarrel sequence shows trouble between friends, in contrast to Brutus's earlier trouble with himself. From Shakespeare's own day up to our own this quarrel has been considered one of the most exciting episodes in the play. Leonard Digges, writing in 1640, says:

So I have seen, when Caesar would appear,
And on the stage at halfe-sword parley were
Brutus and Cassius: oh how the Audience
Were ravish'd, with what wonder they went thence . . .

but the excitement of seeing Cassius and Brutus come to the edge of fighting each other is only one aspect of a varied and deeply moving scene. In a human sense it is the warmest episode in a play which many have considered cold compared to the other tragedies. The clash of personalities, the warmth of reconciliation, the pathos of Portia's death, the quiet council dominated by the ever certain Brutus, and finally darkness, music, silence and the warning apparition—it is a sequence not merely to excite but to stir the mind, the heart, and the imagination, and to educate them all as only Shakespeare at his greatest can.

In the quarrel itself the warmth and vulnerability of Cassius must bring one closer to him than ever before. Indeed there is a danger that the cold insulting righteousness of Brutus may alienate the audience from him in favour of Cassius. This danger is enhanced if we consider the bitter irony of the quarrel about money. Brutus cannot dirty his hands by raising money. He accuses Cassius of dishonest dealings in finance. But how will the noble Brutus get the cash he needs to pay the troops? By getting it from Cassius who has raised it by ignoble means, and by being very angry when Cassius will not pay over a share of his ill-gotten funds!

The actor who takes the part of Brutus must be careful, then, not to act the intolerant prig. If it is clear that Brutus, too, is hurt and angry (as he admits) it will help a great deal; and if this leads into his revelation of Portia's death; and if, here, he shows a touch of deep grief in spite of his stoicism, then the audience will be won over to sympathy.

Mention of Portia brings us to the difficulty of the second dialogue with Messala about her death. If this is acted out after the earlier talk with Cassius, it will seem that Shakespeare is giving us a Brutus capable of lying about his wife's death so as to be given the opportunity of showing off how fine a stoic he is: a repellent exhibition. However commentators are generally agreed that here we have a genuine textual confusion. What seems to have happened is this: in an early version of the play, after the expulsion of the poet, Lucius brought the drink as soon as he was asked, and the friends drank to the end of their quarrel. Thus the whole episode (IV, 3, 143–157 with lines 164–5) in which Brutus tells Cassius about Portia, was not yet written. So the Messala episode is Shakespeare's *earliest* way of dealing with the Portia news. Later, Shakespeare, perhaps because of the coldness with which he had made Brutus receive the news, wrote the Brutus-Cassius revelation, meaning it to *replace* the Messala episode. This can be easily done by cutting from lines 180 to 194, which works very neatly:

MESSALA: Cicero is dead,
And by that order of proscription.
(Thoughtful and rather horrified pause out of which
Brutus firmly brings them back to active business;)

BRUTUS: Well to our work alive.

Messala's 'dead' links up cleanly with Brutus's 'alive'. That both episodes got into the folio by accident or ignorance seems a likely theory, and preferable to believing that Shakespeare meant Brutus to use his wife's death to show off his courage and calm.

The ending of the scene, after Cassius and the others have gone, shows Brutus at his best, gentle and considerate to his followers and humanly frightened but also brave in face of the ghost.

The ghost's enigmatic words 'Thy evil spirit, Brutus' have been variously interpreted. Later we shall return briefly to them when we consider the characters of Caesar and Brutus. For the moment it will suffice to note that the ghosts in the tragedies of Seneca, the Roman playwright whom the Elizabethans imitated so much, were messengers of doom and revenge, and Shakespeare is following this convention, as he was also to do in his next tragedy, *Hamlet*.

One of the most effective elements in the whole scene is the sense of impending death and disaster against which we see the more intimate feelings of Brutus and Cassius. The quarrel itself, despite the reconciliation, shows sadly enough how things are disintegrating and darkening. The news of death and approaching enemies, the loss of Portia, and finally the ghost, warn us of coming catastrophe, and provide a dark background against which the humanity of the protagonists shows more clearly and with greater pathos.

stand: halt
greets me well: sends me greetings by a good man
ill officers: bad officials
worthy: significant
satisfied: have things explained to me
full of regard: worthy of respect
resolved: satisfied
familiar instances: signs of friendship
conference: way of talking to
enforcèd ceremony: strained politeness
hollow: insincere
hot at hand: spirited at first
fall their crests: lower their necks
jades: poor quality horses, hacks, nags
sink: fail
the horse in general: all of the cavalry
gently: slowly
sober form: serious manner
be content: be satisfied (what Brutus actually means is 'be quiet, that is enough')
griefs: complaints, grievances
enlarge: speak openly of
charges: commands,—the troops they are in charge of
noted: publicly condemned
praying on his side: taking his part
was slighted off: was scornfully ignored
That every ... comment: that every small fault be condemned
an itching palm: a nature greedy for money
honors: makes seem respectable
And not: except
supporting robbers: protecting or patronising dishonest mercenary officials
And sell ... thus?: and sell our great power, to have and give honour, for as much rubbish (money) as can be held in this way (in the hands)
bay: howl at
bait: harass, tempt to anger
hedge me in: try to control or confine me
conditions: important decisions
urge me no more: do not push me any further
health: physical safety
tempt: provoke
slight: insignificant
rash choler: hasty temper

stares:	glares, looks angry
budge:	give way
observe:	humour
crouch:	bow down before
testy humor:	bad temper
venom of your spleen:	the poison of your anger
waspish:	irritable
vaunting:	boasting
of:	from
moved:	irritated
tempted:	provoked
honesty:	integrity
respect:	notice
indirection:	dishonesty
counters:	coins
rived:	split, broken
alone on Cassius:	on Cassius alone
braved:	bullied
checked:	scolded, corrected
conned by rote:	learnt off by heart
cast into my teeth:	throw into my face, reproach me with
dearer than Pluto's mine:	more precious than all the treasures to be found in the earth (Pluto was the god of the earth and of everything under the earth)
scope:	permission
dishonor shall be humor:	your rude behaviour will be considered simply a mood
enforcèd:	provoked
straight:	immediately
When grief . . . vexeth him:	when sorrows and bad health and moods trouble him
chides:	scolds
leave you so:	not take any notice of you
grudge:	quarrel
cynic:	deliberately rude philosopher
Saucy:	insolent
I'll know . . . his time:	I will allow him his moods when he can choose the right time to show them
jigging:	rhyming, verse-writing
companion:	a term of contempt for a low fellow
give place:	give way
accidental evils:	chance bad luck
crossed:	opposed, contradicted
upon:	as a result of

impatient of:	unable to bear
tidings:	news
distract:	mad
call in question:	consider
power:	army
Bending their expedition:	moving rapidly towards
selfsame tenure:	the same news or meaning
That by . . . outlawry:	public condemnation
bills of outlawry:	public lists of those now condemned as outside the law
once:	at some time
in art:	in theory
alive:	with energy (Pun: 'alive', as opposed to the dead people they have been speaking of)
presently:	immediately
offense:	damage, harm
of force:	necessarily
Do stand . . . affection:	are only faithful to us by force of circumstance
new-added:	newly reinforced
under your pardon:	excuse me (he will not listen to Cassius)
Omitted:	if they fail to do so
bound in:	confined by, limited by
ventures:	what we risk (the image follows the sea imagery we have had so far, and was often used for ships sent out with merchandise to try to make a trading profit)
with your will:	as you choose
niggard:	pay off meanly or cheaply
hence:	go from this place
gown:	dressing gown
Never come:	may there never come
instrument:	musical instrument (in Rome it would have been a lyre, but on the Elizabethan stage it was almost certainly a lute)
knave:	young fellow, boy
o'erwatched:	weary for want of sleep
raise:	wake
watch your pleasure:	be ready to do what you want
otherwise bethink me:	change my mind
And touch . . . or two:	and play a tune or two on your instrument
an't:	if it
young bloods:	youthful constitutions
murd'rous:	having an appearance like death

leaden mace:	leaden means heavy, the mace was a ceremonial club often carried before those in high office as a symbol of their power, legal or civil (sleep thus has a heavy power over the boy)
How ill this taper burns:	how badly this candle burns (candles are supposed to burn dim or blue in the presence of a ghost or spirit)
upon:	towards
stare:	stand on end
false:	out of tune
commend me:	give my regards to
Bid him . . . before:	tell him to get his forces moving off quickly in advance

Act V Scene 1: Confrontation

(Private conference. Public scene. Private. Medium length. Morning. Some days later on the plains of Philippi.)

We return to Antony and Octavius, whom we find preparing for battle against the approaching forces of their enemies. In a short but significant exchange, Octavius, the young Augustus Caesar, shows his grand-uncle's imperial spirit by calmly refusing Antony's orders and insisting on leading the right (senior) wing of the army.

Then Brutus and Cassius march on stage with their vanguard and there is a fine exchange of characteristic boasting and insults between the leaders of the opposing armies.

Antony and Octavius challenge the others to meet them immediately on the field of battle and withdraw to prepare for the fight.

The scene ends on a quiet note of foreboding and farewell. Cassius tells Messala of his fears and of the evil omens that have followed the armies of the conspirators. Then Brutus and Cassius speak for the last time. Their spirits are low and they talk of defeat and death, but their parting is affectionate and courageous.

NOTES AND GLOSSARY:

As far as the story is concerned this scene is a preparation for the last battle and final catastrophe. There is the excitement and mounting suspense of the confrontation of the two pairs of leaders, a confrontation that brings out the dignity and steady pride of Brutus, the stinging temper of Cassius which is matched by the fierce hatred of Antony's accusations, and finally the ringing challenges to fate and enemies from young Octavius.

Notice, as they quarrel, how the name of Caesar, repeated again and again, invokes his presence and power on this last battlefield. Perhaps it is a sense of this presence that so subdues the spirits of Brutus and Cassius at the end of the scene. For all their courage they talk like condemned men.

Shakespeare has condensed the whole battle sequence in his usual way, but he has also made one real change which is of interest in understanding his intention and technique. In Plutarch it was Brutus who insisted on commanding the right wing of the conspirators' army and who overruled Cassius. Had Shakespeare shown this, it would, of course, have further reinforced those earlier impressions of Brutus's dominance so steadily built up through the play. Why then did he transfer it to Octavius and Antony? Several reasons may be suggested. He may have wanted to avoid any further clash between the reconciled Cassius and Brutus for whom he enlists our warmest and most personal sympathies at their last farewell. In overruling Cassius before, moreover, Brutus was always wrong—but here Brutus's leading of the right wing is, up to a point, successful, and thus would break the pattern of the play. Also Shakespeare uses the transferred argument to show the growing contrast and clash between Antony and Octavius. It is as though he were already feeling his way towards his *Antony and Cleopatra* in which that contrast and clash, and that psychological dominance of the young Caesar over Antony, form one of the major tensions of the play.

battles:	armies
warn:	challenge
demand:	bring to action
in their bosoms:	understand their plans, know their thoughts
visit other places:	be somewhere else
fearful bravery:	fear inspiring show of courage
face:	display, pretence
fasten in our thoughts:	impress us
bloody sign:	red flag
lead your battle softly on:	advance your army slowly
even:	level
Why do you cross me . . . exigent:	why do you oppose me in this situation
answer on their charge:	wait until they attack
posture of your blows:	the way you can strike
Hybla:	a place in Sicily, famous for its honey
you showed your teeth like apes:	the monkey tribe grin when they are angry and about to attack, as the conspirators smiled at Caesar before killing him
might have ruled:	could have had it his own way
cause:	the action we are here for

proof: test
sword goes up: that the sword will be sheathed
another Caesar: that is, himself
have added slaughter to: has also been killed by
strain: family, stock
peevish: foolishly bad-tempered
worthless: not worthy of
reveler: dissipated man
when you have stomachs: when you have the appetite to, when you want to
on the hazard: at risk
set: stake, risk
that I held Epicurus strong: that I believed firmly in what Epicurus said. (Epicurus thought that there was no meaning in omens because there was no divine pattern to be found in the lives of men.)
presage: foreshadow, foretell
former ensign: foremost banner or standard
fell: swooped down
consorted: came with
sickly: ready for death
a canopy most fatal: in the richer Elizabethan beds there were four posts in the corners which supported a cloth over the bed, a canopy, and curtains which could be drawn around the sides. The shadow of the birds over the army is compared to the shadow of the bed canopy over a dying man.
constantly: steadily, bravely
lovers: close friends
incertain: unsure, uncertain
befall: happen
that philosophy: Stoicism, which encouraged suicide rather than dishonour
fall: happen
prevent: forestall
time: term, end
To stay the providence: to wait for the decision (on when was the right time for him to die)
triumph: the procession of victory through Rome of any successful general, in which his prisoners would be led as chained captives
sufficeth: is enough

Act V Scene 2: Brutus in action

In this short linking scene we see Brutus shortly afterwards delivering the orders for a charge against Octavius's forces.

NOTES AND GLOSSARY:
On the Shakespearean stage the whole of this Act of battle and defeat would be one continuous flow of action with little or no pause between the scenes: the flexible nature of Elizabethan stage conventions of space and time would allow a continuity of action.

Alarum: a battle signal made by trumpets or drums
bills: written papers, dispatches, battle orders
other side: the other wing of his own army, commanded by Cassius
cold demeanor: Octavius's troops seemed unwilling to fight, dispirited
push: attack

Act V Scene 3: The death of Cassius

(*Private conference and then Public scene. Medium length. Shortly after, at sunset, on the battlefield.*)

Cassius and Titinius come in, following their retreating troops. Antony has overthrown their wing of the army. Cassius is in rage and despair, carrying a standard that he has taken from a fleeing ensign-bearer whom he has killed for running away. Their battle plans have gone wrong. Brutus's troops, victorious over Octavius, have lost discipline and are looting instead of coming to the help of Cassius's men.

Cassius will retreat no farther. He goes up a little hill and, seeing some troops nearby, sends Titinius to find out if they are friend or foe. Pindarus is to watch Titinius from farther up the hill and tell Cassius how he fares, for Cassius is short-sighted.

From a few words of soliloquy spoken by Cassius, as he waits for news, it is clear that he has abandoned himself to a sense of fate. He is sure that this, his birthday, is to be the day of his death.

Pindarus calls from above: he can see Titinius surrounded by horsemen. He thinks, wrongly, that they are enemies and that they have captured Titinius.

The news that his friend has been taken prisoner is the final blow to the passionate Cassius. He calls Pindarus down and orders him to hold his sword, the sword that struck Caesar, so that he can fall on it and kill himself. He dies in error and excited grief with Caesar's name on his lips. Pindarus, very sensibly, escapes while he can.

And now Titinius returns with Messala. The men he met on the battlefield were the victorious Brutus and his staff. He has come to give good news of the other part of the battle, and to crown Cassius with a wreath of victory sent by Brutus. He finds the body of his leader and friend, guesses what has happened, speaks a fine epitaph:

'The sun of Rome is set. Our day is gone . . .'

Messala goes to tell Brutus the fatal news. Titinius, left alone crowns the dead Cassius and, overcome with grief, kills himself with Cassius's sword. Brutus comes and finds the dead:

O, Julius Caesar thou art mighty yet!
Thy spirit walks abroad, and turns our swords
In our own proper entrails.

He cannot weep yet for Cassius. After brief arrangements for the funeral he orders his troops into battle again.

NOTES AND GLOSSARY:
The death of Cassius is completely in character. Moody, nervous, passionate, and affectionate, he falls victim to his own feelings and delusions. The death of Titinius is a tribute to all that is best in Cassius, including his need for friendship. So are the few but moving words spoken by Brutus over the bodies.

Cassius dies suitably in the red rays of the setting sun. The passing of his fiery spirit is matched by the sky; just as Brutus, the thoughtful man, the late-walking solitary night-reader, dies in darkness; just as Caesar at the height of his glory dies in the blaze of mid-day.

In the treatment of the battle scene which he found in Plutarch Shakespeare has compressed and simplified the material in his usual way. He has also chosen a more stageable form of death than that reported in his source, where it is set down that Pindarus, on Cassius's instructions, struck off the head of his master!

the villains fly:	that is, his own troops are running away
ensign:	standard-bearer
it:	the battle-standard
spoil:	loot
far:	farther
yond:	those
with a thought:	as quick as thought

My sight was ever thick: I have always been shortsighted
is run his compass: has completed its circuit, has run its race
make to him on the spur: ride towards him spurring their horses for speed

light:	dismount
ta'en:	taken, captured
swore:	made you swear
saving of:	when saving
search:	pierce, penetrate
stand:	wait
change:	exchange, tit-for-tat
dews:	considered unhealthy and infectious, also a metaphor for tears
Mistrust of:	doubts about
O hateful Error, Melancholy's child:	melancholy men were supposed to be wrapped up in their own thoughts and often the victims of their own imaginary fears
apt:	impressionable
mother:	that is the person who conceives the error
Hie:	hurry
misconstrued:	misinterpreted
hold thee:	wait
apace:	quickly
regarded:	honoured
this is a Roman's part:	the Stoic duty of suicide
own proper:	very own
brave:	noble
whe'r:	whether
fellow:	equal
moe:	more
Thasos:	an island near Philippi
discomfort:	discourage

Act V Scene 4: The battle lost

(*Public scene. Short. Towards nightfall on the battlefield.*)

Brutus and his men are fighting bravely but are being beaten. Brutus leaves the stage with some followers. Young Cato dies heroically. Lucilius is surrounded and pretends to be Brutus, to give his leader a better chance of escape. He demands death, but is captured and handed over to Antony who knows him. Lucilius tells Antony that he will never capture Brutus alive. Antony treats him with generous courtesy, and orders the search for Brutus to continue.

NOTES AND GLOSSARY:
Fate is closing in on Brutus also. The courage of Cato and the devotion of Lucilius are tributes to him and his cause as his end approaches.

bastard doth not?:	Cato implies that a man must have bad blood, that is, be no true Roman if he will not keep up his courage. This Cato is Portia's brother and equally proud of his parentage.
Only I yield . . . straight:	Lucilius says he will only surrender if they will kill him, when he says, 'There is so much', he may be offering them money to kill him, or he may be saying there is so much against Brutus that their only choice is to kill him.
straight:	immediately
like himself:	behaving characteristically
is chanced:	has turned out

Act V Scene 5: The death of Brutus

(*Private conference and then Public scene. Medium length. A little later, at night, near the battlefield.*)

Brutus comes in with a few survivors of his army. They rest, and Brutus asks them one by one to hold his sword so that he may kill himself. In horror and grief they refuse. Brutus is sad but steady. He praises his friends and bids them farewell. As the enemy approach is heard, he persuades all except Strato to escape. After taking his leader's hand Strato holds the sword, and Brutus, falling on it, speaks his last words:

> 'Caesar, now be still;
> I killed not thee with half so good a will.'

Antony and Octavius enter in triumph with their forces and with Messala and Lucilius as prisoners. Strato is found and questioned about Brutus. He shows them the body and Lucilius praises and thanks the dead Brutus for being true to himself.

A mood of quietness and generosity possesses victors and vanquished. Octavius offers service to all who have served Brutus and takes Strato into his household on Messala's recommendation.

Antony has been standing or kneeling, looking at the body of the man who may have loved Caesar even as well as he, Antony, did, and whom Caesar loved even more than he loved Antony. Now that Brutus is dead, Antony can and must pay tribute to him, 'the noblest Roman of them all', who killed Caesar not in envy but for the public good. A man perfect in every way.

Octavius takes command. The body of Brutus shall lie in state in his tent for the night while the victory is celebrated and the victors rest.

NOTES AND GLOSSARY:
This scene is in many ways a twin to the death scene of Cassius: the

retreating men, the worsening news, the theme of death and friendship; the suicide itself with death on the name of Caesar; the discovery of the body; the last tributes.

However, largely because of the different character of Brutus, but partly also because of the hopeless peace of final defeat, it is a far quieter scene. Brutus's private moments have all been nightpieces, and so is this, which adds to the sense of stillness, almost of release:

Night hangs upon mine eyes; my bones would rest,
That have but laboured to attain this hour.

By now it will be clear that one of the great themes of the play is friendship. The reconciliation, in the death of one of Caesar's two greatest friends, brings a final warmth to the play, and to Brutus's end. The play draws to a close in solemn and stately tones, but there is little of the terror and pity of the great tragedies.

It is fascinating to see how, even in this generous ending, this tribute of enemies, Shakespeare further reinforces his creation of the contrast between Octavius and Antony. Octavius is looking for reliable followers and knows he may find them among the friends of the dead man. He is asserting himself: *he* will take charge, the body of Brutus will lie in *his* tent. Antony, on the other hand, thinks of the dead and of the spirit of noble men; he makes only one speech, his praise of his dead enemy.

remains:	survivors
showed the torchlight:	gave an arranged signal by waving a torch (he had been sent to see if Cassius's camp had been overrun by the other army)
Now is . . . eyes:	Brutus is compared to the small urns in which the tears of the mourners were gathered as a tribute to the dead
list:	listen to
several:	separate
pit:	a pun: first it means a trap for wild animals into which they are driven; and, secondly, it means the tomb or the grave
vile conquest:	ignoble victory
at once:	immediately
That have . . . hour:	that have only worked their way through life to reach the final resting place at the hour of death
respect:	reputation
smatch:	taste, trace
man:	servant, slave
For Brutus . . . himself:	only Brutus could conquer himself
Lucilius' saying:	that is, that Brutus would be found like himself

entertain them: take them under my protection, employ them in my service

bestow: spend

prefer: recommend

latest: last

envy: malice, hatred

general honest thought/And common good to all: an honest concern for the public good

made one of them: joined them

gentle: noble

and the elements/So mixed in him: it was held that man's temperament was decided by the way that the four elements of earth, water, air and fire were mingled in his physical make-up: so Brutus is supposed to have been a finely balanced mixture to make a noble person

virtue: quality, excellence

use: treat

most like a soldier: according to the honourable customs of a military funeral

the field: the soldiers still in action on the field of battle

part: divide

Finis: (*Latin*) the end

Part 3

Commentary

Critical approaches to the play

The critic George Watson has said that there are three ways in which we can approach a Shakespearean play: we can consider the structure, the way the play is put together, the way it moves and develops; we can consider the people in the play, the dramatic characters; and finally we can try to find out how the play works in terms of the language and the poetry. To these we should add the consideration of the play as theatre, as something essentially to be acted: a script not a book.

Of course these apparently different approaches are really part of the same exploration and enjoyment; and so each will, or should, lead us to the others. Language creates character, character is the basis of action, of dramatic structure.

Structures

It has been said already that Shakespeare took pains to make *Julius Caesar* a play worthy of its great subject. It bears all the marks of a careful, even mathematical construction; so that in some ways it is far *neater* than most of Shakespeare's dramas.

Patterns of action

In the main, the play follows a time-honoured narrative pattern which has been used for hundreds of years. The principal character, in this case Brutus, is brought into conflict with a problem, which involves a struggle with either circumstances, other people, or himself, or with any combination of these three. In *Julius Caesar* the problem of Caesar's power involves Brutus in all these forms of conflict: he tries to decide what he should do, he argues with Cassius and Portia, he struggles with his own thoughts and feelings. This part of a story or play in which the conflict is made clear to us, and often also to the protagonist, is usually called the EXPOSITION and often corresponds to Act I of a five act play.

After the exposition we come to the DEVELOPMENT in which the hero plans and takes decisive action to solve his problem. This usually corresponds in a five act play to Act II, and this is so in *Julius Caesar*, for in Act II Brutus decides that Caesar must die, takes charge of the conspirators, and adopts their immediate plan of action, which they begin by calling on Caesar and persuading him to come to the Senate House.

Now comes the CLIMAX or CRISIS brought about by the hero's action. This crisis, exciting in itself, brings to light a new element in the situation, of which the hero had been ignorant and which frustrates his solution, bringing him face to face with an even more severe challenge. The death of Caesar is immediately followed by the counter-thrust of Antony's action. Brutus not only fails to recognise the danger of Antony, he fails, much more fatally, to realise that the new dangers of Caesarism cannot be simply cancelled out by killing Caesar, who may in some ways be a symptom of changes in Rome herself rather than the cause of those changes. The CLIMAX of *Julius Caesar* is only structurally unusual in that it is like a wave with a double crest: it has *two* great scenes, the death of Caesar and the funeral. The two peak moments, are the stabbing and Antony's uncovering of the body in front of the mob. Thus the counterstroke is made of equal dramatic power to the hero's own decisive action.

Act IV, as is usual, shows us the REDEVELOPMENT as the hero again comes to grips with a situation now even more complex and difficult, and in Act V we reach the CATASTROPHE (from a Greek term meaning the unknotting or unravelling) in which the conflict is finally resolved one way or the other. To match the double climax of the play, *Julius Caesar* gives us a double catastrophe in the twin death-scenes of Cassius and Brutus.

Patterns of scene and theme

To match the formal neatness of the main action there are various other patterns to give *Julius Caesar* a strong orderly development. There is a balance of short and long scenes which gives us a constant weaving of crowd, group, pair and single figure. By turning to the short notes in brackets at the beginning of each scene as it is dealt with above, it can be seen how systematic Shakespeare has been in these arrangements. The alternation between public and private scenes reveals the central thematic development of the play, which is shown to concern itself with the conflict between public and private life, between the duties of the citizen and feelings and obligations of the private person. A diagram on page 68 gives the rhythm of this conflict as shown in the arrangement of the play. The word 'respublica', literally the people's thing, is chosen here because in Rome it meant the commonweal, the public good, the state itself; and because it is, of course, the root of the word republic.

Thus it stands for all those things for which Brutus gave the life of his friends, and then his own life.

Respublica I,1	troubles my mind I,2
Respublica I,3	troubles my heart II,1
Inevitable II,2,3 & 4	death III,1
Inevitable III,1	reaction III,2 & 3
Respublica IV,1	troubles my spirit IV,2 & 3
Inevitable V,1 & 2	death V,3
Dark V,4	death V,5

Patterns of time

Structures of action, staging and theme are further reinforced by what may be called structures of time. 'Short' and 'long' time in Shakespeare's plays has already been discussed in the notes to II,1; but, looking at the play as a whole, we find a completely tidy arrangement of three 'stage days' from morning until night.

The first day: in the morning the citizens take to the streets to celebrate, in the afternoon the Lupercal race is run while Cassius talks to Brutus, in the evening and as night closes in there are storms and portents, and that night Brutus meets the conspirators at his house and joins the plot.

The second day: next morning they bring Caesar to the Capitol, at noon they kill him, that afternoon at the funeral Antony raises the mob to rebellion. That evening the triumvirs meet in their headquarters, while in Sardis Brutus and Cassius first quarrel and then plan a battle.

The third day: in the morning the armies meet, in the afternoon the battle begins, as the sun sets Cassius kills himself, as night falls the battle is lost, in the dark of that night Brutus dies.

Although this time scheme is historically impossible it has quite the opposite effect on the stage. What the audience get is a sense of the *natural passage of time* through the revolutions of night and day. The sense of changing hours satisfies our experience, particularly as Shakespeare uses the different times of the day and night with both realism and imagination. The rhythms of real life, of human beings caught in the recurring wheel of light and dark help to draw us into the world of the play. The powerful patterns of ordinary life are one of the central sources of Shakespeare's poetic strength.

Patterns of character

Later the individual characters in the play will be considered, but, while pattern is being discussed, we should notice that in the arrangement of characters within the play Shakespeare has followed again a very symmetrical balance and one which tells us about the nature of the play. When we arrange the characters of other tragedies into patterns which mirror the dramatic tensions of the plays, we find, hardly surprisingly, that the hero is at the centre of these arrangements. The other characters in the play are balanced around the protagonist in various ways. In some sense the mind and character of the hero contain all the other people in the play. As Maynard Mack* has said the play is in some sense the world as seen through the eyes of the hero.

When we try to apply this to Brutus in *Julius Caesar* we find that it does not work at all well. Brutus may be the nearest thing we have to a tragic hero in the play but he is not central enough to the structure or vision of the work to be considered a full tragic hero. It is when we put Caesar himself in the centre that the light dawns and we see clearly a manifestation of that balance in the play which makes its title *Julius Caesar* and not *Marcus Brutus*.

CAESAR

BRUTUS   ANTONY

CASSIUS   OCTAVIUS

This little scheme of the main characters will show—to put it most simply—that Caesar has two friends who contrast with each other in almost every way, and that each of these friends has a friend who in his turn contrasts with him. Brutus is Caesar's cold friend, and so Brutus has a hot friend, Cassius. Antony is Caesar's hot friend and so he acquires a cold friend, Octavius. Caesar himself possesses the qualities that we find in *all the others*. The play is about his world even though, as we have seen in our analysis of the action, Brutus is the tragic protagonist.

---

*Maynard Mack, 'The Jacobean Shakespeare: Some Observations on the Construction of the Tragedies', *Stratford-on-Avon Studies: Jacobean Theatre* (Vol. I) ed. Brown and Harris (1960).

Some critics have reacted unfavourably to the division of the drama between Caesar and Brutus. Caesar is the most commanding, if not the most interesting figure in the play and he, against all the rules, is killed half-way through. How can the play possibly recover from the loss of power that must result from the loss of Caesar? Such critics have claimed, more or less emphatically, that it does not in fact recover, and that the last two acts never really rise to the same level as the first three.

The answer to this is that Caesar is most important in the play not so much as a person but as a force: a power over the ideas and actions of the others. Critics who believe in the success of the play have pointed out that, though Caesar dies, he so fills the rest of the play with his presence that he determines the whole action. Brutus wishes that the conspirators could kill the spirit of Caesarism without injuring the body of Caesar; in fact what they do is exactly the opposite, for after his death his influence, his spirit, his name, and his ghost fill the rest of the play, so:

> . . . Caesar's spirit, ranging for revenge,
> With Ate by his side, come hot from hell,
> Shall in these confines with a monarch's voice
> Cry 'Havoc!' and let slip the dogs of war . . .

So the play is divided between Caesar and Brutus, and this does make it different from, though not necessarily inferior to, other tragedies. Acts IV and V are particularly affected and the catastrophe does not rise to the same heights as the crisis in the climax of Act III. However, this does not mean that the end of the play is a failure; the ending is inevitable, right, and effective, and no-one who sees the play well acted will feel any sense of falling-off or disappointment at the end. There is no sacred rule that says that the catastrophe of a play must be more intense than the climax, provided that it is interesting in itself and that it proceeds strongly from the earlier action.

As has been suggested, if Caesar is considered to be a power as much as a person, Shakespeare's dramatic intention and success will be better understood than by wrangling about who is the 'central character'. So the story of the struggle of Brutus against the Caesar phenomenon could be called *Marcus Brutus* or *Julius Caesar*. In passing, it should be recognised that the name which Shakespeare chose is far better for a box-office.

A note on the nature of the action

Julius Caesar is cleanly and strongly made, and its clear lines of construction are matched by the energy of the action. As we shall see, when we consider the language of the play, this is a lively composition, full of a forceful heroic atmosphere which celebrates courage, friendship and generosity of spirit. In many ways it is more accurate to call it epic than tragic.

Character

First, a few general remarks about Shakespeare's creation of dramatic character and about the particular problems of character in *Julius Caesar*.

Shakespeare is one of the great masters of character creation. The depth, variety, and complexity of the people in his plays has never been surpassed by either dramatist or novelist. He has so persuaded many people of the reality of these characters that many books of Shakespeare criticism have been written which treat the characters in the plays as if they were indeed real men and women, whose thoughts, ideas and actions had all the consistency and depth of real life. For many theatre-goers and readers, a Hamlet, a Falstaff or a Cleopatra seem more real indeed than the people who live next door.

To take an example, A. C. Bradley, when discussing *Hamlet* in his justly famous *Shakespearean Tragedy*, talks about Hamlet's 'inner healthy self which doubtless in time would have fully reasserted itself'. But Hamlet has no inner self at all, healthy or unhealthy; Hamlet is a part in the play of that name, not a real person.

Much of our enjoyment of the plays does consist, indeed, in co-operating with Shakespeare's astonishing imagination and 'suspending our disbelief' so far as to react to the story as if it were in some sense true. The plays, to use Shakespeare's own image, are a mirror of human nature and we can not only enjoy them but also learn from them. But we must be careful about putting forward our own theories and imaginative extensions of our experience of the play as if these were something that Shakespeare himself had invented, instead of being our personal tribute to the way he has set our own imaginations to work.

A play, particularly a Shakespearean play, is not even a novel in which the author may invite us to share the certainties of knowing about the 'real' feelings and thoughts of the characters. In a play we have speech and action which imply or express thought and feeling, but we cannot arrive at the inner consciousness of the characters. Even in soliloquy there is not the same certainty as when for instance the novelist tells us that some character 'felt deeply sad', or 'felt his spirits lift', or so on.

A character in a play is *a part to be played*, and it can often be played in various ways. Different actors give us different Brutuses, different Cassiuses. If the actor is good his interpretation of a part will be a kind of blend of things in himself with what he has found in the play.

What, then, does the actor or the producer—or the reader for that matter—look for when he seeks to arrive at his own satisfactory and valid interpretation of a character? There is what the character himself does and says, including what he says about himself; and there is also his effect on other people, what he causes them to do and to say, including what they say about him either to his face or to other people in the play. By studying these things in a Shakespeare play we arrive often at a mass of evidence about a character, often very complex, and even contradictory.

Shakespeare's Romans

Shakespeare approached the subject of Julius Caesar with great caution and respect. Renaissance Europe looked back on the Greeks and Romans as the absolute pattern of civilization. The Greeks were the models of thought and art, the Romans were admired for order and law. The name Rome stood for power, empire, rule and achievement. Shakespeare followed his main source in Plutarch with great care, bringing what he found there to extended dramatic life but very seldom taking any major liberties with the main facts or characters.

He was obviously extremely careful about the tone and style of the play. Ben Jonson and other neo-classical writers, who took their models from Greek and Roman writers, believed in a decorum or right rule of style in which a high subject shoud be treated in a high style, and in *Julius Caesar* even Shakespeare, who is usually far freer in style than, say, Jonson, seems to have cultivated a high ringing rhetorical tone with no lapses into vulgarity, and indeed few into ordinary everyday speech.

All the people in *Julius Caesar*, then, talk in high-sounding noble phrases and this gives the play its ringing 'Roman' quality, but it also has a negative effect. Such care about correct speech and about stately noble manner creates a distance between the audience and the people in the play. Even Portia, for instance, a wife lovingly reproving her husband, talks rather as if she were addressing the Roman Senate:

> I grant I am a woman; but withal
> A woman that Lord Brutus took to wife.
> I grant I am a woman; but withal
> A woman well reputed, Cato's daughter.
> Think you I am no stronger than my sex,
> Being so fathered and so husbanded?

The result of this grand manner is a certain coldness about the play despite its excitement and energy. Many critics have noticed this and even Dr Johnson, with his deep classical training, remarked:

> . . . I have never been strongly agitated in persuing it (*Julius Caesar*) and think it somewhat cold and unaffecting compared with some other of Shakespeare's plays; his adherence to the real story and to Roman manners seems to have impeded the natural vigour of his genius. (from the Notes to his edition of Shakespeare, 1765).

Caesar

Attitudes to Caesar of which Shakespeare would have known were as ambivalent as his own approach in the play. In his study of the books which influenced Shakespeare Geoffrey Bullough has pointed out that the historians and other writers of Renaissance times showed complex and even contrasting reactions not only to Caesar but also to the conspirators and to Antony. In sixteenth century writings Caesar himself appeared a man of paradox:

> On the one hand there was general agreement on his martial skill, energy, eloquence, power over his legions and the plebeians; on his kindness to his friends and soldiers, his moderation in diet, his frequent clemency. On the other hand he was widely regarded as capable of great ruthlessness, a despiser of religion, lustful, guileful, and above all ambitious. (Geoffrey Bullough, *Narrative and Dramatic Sources of Shakespeare, V*)

Shakespeare took dramatic advantage of the paradox to the extent that the play is really based on the different possible attitudes to Caesar: think only of the funeral orations of Brutus and Antony. In the man, Caesar himself, whom he represents to us, we also have a realistic and fertile ambiguity. To maintain balance and realism he makes a Caesar less evil than the portrait given by Plutarch. Shakespeare shows again and again in his plays his knowledge of the complexity of human nature, and this world-conqueror is seen in the play under most of the aspects, both good and bad, listed above by Bullough, except for 'lustful'.

Shakespeare also shows us an ageing man, subject to epilepsy, deaf in one ear, possibly nervous of rebellion despite his proud words about danger and fear, certainly an easy victim to flattery such as that used so openly by Decius to get him to come to the Senate.

But above all the Caesar of the play is a great man, a man of power and pride—of overweening pride. Even when allowance is made for the Elizabethan convention which permits a person in a play to speak openly of his own character, good or bad, we still have something excessive in the way that this Caesar talks of himself. He describes himself as a lion, as Mount Olympus, as the Northern Star: images of a god-like greatness.

But again the portrait is warmed by touches of kindness and humanity: his concern for his wife, the cheerful hospitality to his visitors on the morning of his death, his good humoured affection for Antony, and, at the very end, the shock he suffers in seeing his other dear friend, Brutus, among his killers.

Above all he is most important in the play as a power over other men's feelings, actions, and ideas. The various voices of the play speak more of him even when he is dead than of any other character, even Brutus. For good and ill the words of Cassius remain true:

> Why, man, he doth bestride the narrow world
> Like a Colossus, and we petty men
> Walk under his huge legs and peep about
> To find ourselves dishonourable graves. (I,2).

In the history plays Shakespeare had been exploring concepts and images of power in men and was to continue to do so in the tragedies, though here his interest was shifting from the group or nation to the individual. One key aspect of other explorations is missing in Caesar; the idea of kingship as a holy office. Caesar's power, in a pagan Roman world, is purely secular, compared, for example, to the reverence and awe that surrounds the good king Duncan in Shakespeare's *Macbeth*. There is a sense of sacrilege surrounding his death. Caesar's death is not shown, like Duncan's, as a religious offense, but as an offense against friendship and against order, and as such is dreadful enough. The results of the deed on the men who did it and on the commonweal are disastrous. Shakespeare shows that the overthrow of even a corrupt power by violent means is a terrible and dangerous undertaking.

An imperfect world gives power to imperfect men. Caesar, ambiguous and complex, 'all things to all men' as a contemporary said of him, is absolute in one thing only, his belief in himself, in his right to rule, in his greatness: 'For always I am Caesar'. This is his power and also his *hubris*, his fatal and mighty pride . . . It is in this pride, in this absolute belief in himself that he resembles Brutus.

Brutus

In giving us the character of Brutus Shakespeare faced in its most acute form the problem of his noble Romans. A hero so calm, so brave, so unflinching as to be very nearly dull. Stoicism, of its very nature, is *undramatic*.

The Stoic philosophy originated in Greece with the teachings of Zeno. It held that happiness consisted in freeing oneself from the slavery of emotion and appetite, and in serving virtue. The good life was one of calm detachment from everything except one's duty. Suffering was a matter of indifference. It was in Rome that this philosophy took strongest root:

> 'The impact of Stoicism upon Roman temperament and tradition forms a striking chapter in the development of morality. The system was of Greek invention, tinged with some colouring of Eastern intuitions, yet it did not, on any large scale, become a moral force, until it migrated and acclimatised itself at Rome. There, as by some predetermined harmony, it found the soil and antecedents suited to its growth, and became a fructifying power in the future of civilisation. The Roman thought of duty, as expressed in *virtus*—Manliness, the Roman instinct for law, and the Roman sense of religion—binding, omnipresent, impersonal—found a meeting-place in the Stoic creed . . . The self-repression and austerity of type, the subjection of the individual to the whole, the subordination of impulse and affection to the demands of moral obligation, the doggedness and inflexibility of the virtues exercised, all fell in with the ideals of republican virtue.'*

It would be hard to find a better description of Shakespeare's Brutus, or the description of a man harder to make into exciting dramatic material. 'Give me that man who is not passion's slave', says Hamlet passionately, but Hamlet himself is no stoic, but a creature of moods and emotions which he can hardly control; and therefore far, far more exciting on the stage than Brutus. In *Hamlet* Shakespeare kept his stoic, but only as Horatio—a foil and friend for his passionate hero. Horatio even says: 'I am more an antique Roman than a Dane.'

It has been suggested earlier that if Brutus is acted as the perfect Stoic he will be in danger of losing all the sympathy of the audience. There seems to be enough evidence in the play to justify an interpretation of the part as of a young man striving with himself to follow the Stoic ideal and succeeding pretty well, but now and then showing a surge of natural feeling—enough to gain our sympathy and liking: as when Portia's reproaches wring from him the deep avowal:

> You are my true and honourable wife
> As dear to me as are the ruddy drops
> That visit my sad heart.

Or as when, looking at the body of Cassius, he says:

> Friends, I owe more tears
> To this dead man than you shall see me pay.
> I shall find time, Cassius, I shall find time.

*G.H. Rendall, Introduction to Marcus Aurelius Antoninus, *To Himself*, London, 1907, pp. xxv–vi.

Yet in these deeply moving moments we still feel the restraint on feeling: 'drops' of blood, 'sad (with its Elizabethan connotation of serious) heart'; here is no easy flow of feeling; and in the second case we see a man unable or unwilling to weep for his friend in public. Always we find that 'self-repression and austerity.'

In late Victorian times Brutus was much admired. His ability to deal with the corrupt world outside his study might be questioned, but he was almost always seen as the noble patriot, the pattern of selfless integrity. This treatment of him, as Leonard F. Dean has shown,* has changed slowly but radically. Dante, long ago, put Brutus in the demon's mouth in lowest hell for his sin against his prince and friend,† and many twentieth century critics write as if they would agree with this extreme judgement, at least in the case of Shakespeare's Brutus if not of the real man.

It is Brutus's self-confident idealism that has gone out of favour in a century which is justified in suspecting men who kill other men and cause wars in the name of ideals. There is evidence in the play that Shakespeare shared this suspicion. Considered carefully there is something grotesque in Brutus's words:

> Stoop, Romans, stoop,
> And let us bathe our hands in Caesar's blood
> Up to the elbows, and besmear our swords.
> Then walk we forth, even to the market place,
> And waving our red weapons o'er our heads,
> Let's all cry 'Peace, freedom, and liberty!'

In another recent essay‡ on the play Colbert Kearney suggested that the tragedy of Brutus is that he himself falls a victim to those very vices of power for which he killed his friend. He becomes as absolute and as dangerous as Caesar. Caesar may have been absolute for power, while Brutus is absolute for principle, but, for those who suffer and die to satisfy the demands of others, the difference is minimal. There is strong evidence that Shakespeare linked the corruption of Caesar to the character of Brutus as it develops in the play. As Kearney points out in his essay, this gives a deep and special meaning to the Ghost's words, 'Thy evil spirit, Brutus': Caesar, Caesarism, power assumed, for whatever reason, and its almost inevitable effect in corrupting the man who wields it. Thus Kearney sees 'the central action of the play' as 'the interrelation of two men, both of whose careers are generated and destroyed by that same sense of pride, ambition and superiority . . .'

*The English Journal, October 1961. Reprinted in the Signet Classic Julius Caesar, edited by W. and B. Rosen, New York, 1963.
†The Inferno: Canto XXXIV
‡'The Nature of an Insurrection: Shakespeare's Julius Caesar', Studies, Summer 1974.

One of the most telling evidences that this was in the mind of Shakespeare is that the only two people in the play who refer to themselves in the third person are Caesar and Brutus. Each speaks of himself with a sort of admiring awe.

An absolute pride and ambition is often the mark of a great tragic hero, but in the case of Brutus it is generally agreed that he fails to reach the intensity necessary for full tragic stature. To understand this we must return to Stoicism: to the fact that he does not change or learn during the play. The far more formidable and evil Macbeth moves us to pity and terror because he learns who he is and what he has done. Shakespeare did not, perhaps dared not, show us a Brutus shaken or broken by tragic knowledge. There is much nobility and some pathos in Brutus's end, but it is not full tragedy.

Cassius

In the first part of the play there is something in Cassius of the conventional stage villain, the evil angel, the tempter, the Iago. His motives are clear and personal: apart from the fact that he knows that Caesar dislikes and suspects him ('Caesar doth bear me hard'), there is his restless envy: 'Such men as he are never at heart's ease/ Whiles they behold a greater than themselves.' Even his appearance, as described by Caesar is unattractive: 'lean and hungry' with a sarcastic self-mocking smile.

What redeems him is his gift of friendship. He is a passionate and excitable man who hates and loves with equal fervour. Also, as T. S. Dorsch says, 'The death of the object of his hatred seems to liberate more generous instincts in him.'* Particularly in the last two acts his affection for Brutus and Titinius marks him as a sympathetic figure, so much so that, as has been said in the commentary on the quarrel scene, there is a real danger that he will rob Brutus of some of the necessary attention and admiration of the audience. However his moodiness and his death, passionate, impetuous and wrong-headed, which is spoken of as the result of 'hateful Error, Melancholy's child' show him in the medical and dramatic theory of the day as an *unbalanced* man, a lesser creature than Brutus who so dominates him and who is described deliberately as the epitome of self-control and natural balance:

> . . . The elements
> So mixed in him that Nature might stand up
> And say to all the world, 'This was a man!'

Cassius, like the other main characters, is a complex figure, even an

*Introduction to The New Arden *Julius Caesar*, Methuen, London, 1955.

ambiguous one. In spite of his emotionalism and lack of balance he is a man of real abilities. He it is who plans the assassination and gathers and leads a group of trustworthy and determined men up to the moment when Brutus takes over command. His practical sense of politics, as in advising the killing of Antony, and of military matters, as in advising against fighting one decisive battle at Philippi, is superior to that of Brutus. We cannot, then, write him off as a mere emotionalist.

His friendship with Brutus is his fate both good and bad, and he provides the perfect dramatic foil for the sober Brutus.

Antony

As Brutus has his Cassius, so Caesar has his Antony, his passionate, affectionate, unprincipled friend. Antony has been called the 'least Roman' of the main characters and in truth there is something un-Roman, free and easy, even slightly savage in the portrait of this reckless but skilful soldier.

It has been remarked that he does not emerge as a character in the play until the death of Caesar. Brutus, it will be remembered, speaks of him as a 'limb of Caesar' and in a sense he is right, though his belief that Antony will be useless and inactive after Caesar's death is fatally wrong. Brutus makes a common mistake that 'serious' men make about those who are fond of sport and having a good time, he discounts him as a frivolous lightweight. Cassius has a far better idea of his abilities and calls him 'a shrewd contriver' that is, a cunning planner, and says that the deep-rooted love he has for Caesar will make him their dangerous enemy.

It is as though Antony were satisfied, while he serves his great leader, to remain in the background; but Caesar's death brings out different things in all men, and suddenly we see Antony as a great and powerful man, one of Caesar's spiritual heirs, a soldier, a statesman, a magnificent orator, who will rapidly become one of the two greatest men in the Roman world. He brings to his love for Caesar that dash and energy which marks all his actions and feelings.

On the darker side there is his cunning, his fierceness, his gambler's irresponsibility with men's lives. Dorsch, rightly, calls him implacable and ferocious. There is something chilling about the calculated way he deals with Brutus and the conspirators: it is brave and brilliant but it has the deadly feeling of a carefully-laid ambush. The impression of ruthlessness is strengthened at the end of the oration scene, and, even more deeply, in the episode when the triumvirs are trading lives for political reasons, a scene with a real taint of corruption.

As he uses Cassius, so also Shakespeare employs Antony as a deliberate and effective contrast to Brutus. Yet he also shares certain things with Brutus, for in his own way he is as brave and single-hearted. Neither he nor Brutus hesitates or counts the cost once he is sure of what he must do.

There is little doubt that the funeral oration is Antony's greatest scene, and it has been much discussed. One of the most interesting problems about his brilliant speech is his sincerity. He says of himself:

I am no orator, as Brutus is;
But (as you know me all) a plain blunt man
That love my friend . . .
For I have neither wit, nor words, nor worth,
Action nor utterance, nor the power of speech
To stir men's blood; I only speak right on.

He must know the power he is exerting over the mob by exactly those gifts of oratory which he says he lacks. Plutarch tells us that Antony gained 'wonderful love' of the common people and soldiers by treating them as equals and chatting or drinking with them, and in passages like the one quoted Shakespeare is building brilliantly on this comment. Also the real genius of Antony as a demagogue, a popular orator, is that there is an element of truth in what he says; he may be using his real feelings to move the crowd, *but they are his real feelings*, and this is one reason why the crowd and even the audience are brought to share them.

Octavius

The character of the young Octavius, afterwards to be Augustus Caesar, is only lightly sketched in, but the touches of the portrait are sure and skilful. He is cool and watchful even if there is a somewhat youthful uncertainty about his first argument with Antony. His ability to overrule Antony, his adoption of the imperial tone in the challenges before battle and his assumption of control at the end of the last scene all give promise of a formidable successor to the name of Caesar.

Casca

In Act I, Scene 2 we get a fairly full introduction to the character of Casca. Here indeed is a 'plain blunt man'. He is a Cynic, a follower of that school of Greek philosophy of which Diogenes is the most famous example. The cynics had no time for culture, art or learning, and culti-vated a rough, rude direct speech, often to show their scorn of others. The prose description of Caesar and the crown is an example, but indeed almost everything that Casca says in this scene is in the cynic mood.

Casca changes so much in the storm scene in which he meets Cicero

and Cassius that some critics have suggested that Shakespeare, or someone else, has cut the play and squashed several conspirators' parts
together so that Casca has been given later speeches meant for someone
else. There is however no need to seek for any further explanation than
that Shakespeare knew well how men change under the stress of fear
and excitement. It is quite common to see a 'tough character' become
nervous, talkative and excitable as Casca does in circumstances of
danger.

Cicero

Cicero gives us a contrast to the excited Casca and the other young
conspirators. His calm irony and steady dry commonsense help to
emphasise the disturbance and passion of Casca and Cassius.

Portia

In Shakespeare's portrayal of Portia we find again that combination of
nobility, dignity, courage, generosity, and passion which we have
marked in different proportions in his other Romans. This is his
Roman lady, fit wife for his Brutus, as she claims herself. Her beauty
and her vulnerability add a humanity and pathos to the play. Like
Desdemona, Ophelia, Cordelia, and even Lady Macbeth, she is one of
the young women destroyed in the tragedies by involvement with the
fate of the heroes. She is particularly like Ophelia and Lady Macbeth in
that her death is brought about by mental and emotional collapse under
the pressures of the tragic action. There is a fine contrast in her scenes
between the brave steady creature she is determined to be and the deep
groundswell of passion and nervous excitability felt under her words
and actions. The violent situation brings out in her a sort of heroic
hysteria: she wounds her thigh, she swallows fire. She also helps to
provide a warm and sympathetic background for the rather cold
Brutus.

Calphurnia

The other wife in the play, Calphurnia, both contrasts with and parallels
Portia. Granville-Barker calls her a 'nervous fear-haunted creature'.
She is quite unlike Portia in that she has no heroic aspirations for her
husband or herself, but she is like her in that she shows the pressure of
the tragic power game on the nerves and lives of those who love the
politicians.
   Again she is used to give a human dimension to great Caesar's
portrait; and, also, with her dreams and forebodings, she acts the role of
a Cassandra, a weeping prophetess of death and destruction.

Other characters

When we look through the entire *Dramatis Personae*, we may be struck by the way in which Caesar and his friends are outnumbered. There are all those conspirators, all those friends of Brutus and Cassius, all those servants to Brutus. True, three senators are named—but they are either neutral or friendly to the plot against Caesar. Before the late arrival of Octavius and Lepidus, Antony is the only powerful friend of Caesar in the play and we have shown how light his part is kept until after Caesar's death. Apart from him, the early scenes show only one nervous wife, one soothsayer, and one teacher of rhetoric concerned for the safety of Caesar.

Notice has been taken of some of the minor parts in the play in the commentary on the action. Apart from the roles played in the events by minor characters we may recognise that in general they contribute to the warmth of the play: they build up that general feeling of friendship and affection which is one of the marks of the world of *Julius Caesar*. Brutus and Cassius are surrounded by devoted friends and admirers; and, though Caesar may be more isolated, Antony and the crowds make up his share of affection and praise when the time comes.

The play is rich in rapidly sketched individuals who also have the function of interesting us for their own sakes by a sudden flash of character. The austere Cicero has been described: also there are Decius, the skilful and confident flatterer; the solemn, visionary Soothsayer; Ligarius, rousing himself to action out of sickness and depression; Artimedorus trying to struggle through with his warning; trembling old Publius facing the wild bloodstained young men; the servant of Octavius suddenly breaking down at the sight of the dead Caesar; Lepidus trotting off like a good dog when Antony tells him to; Titinius's death; Pindarus running off after helping Cassius to kill himself, in contrast to the taciturn Strato who stays quietly by the body of Brutus after performing the same office for him. These and many other touches of interest and understanding help to build up the human world of the play.

The language of the play

The magic of Shakespeare make us 'believe' in his plays, makes us think that they are 'exactly like real life'. They *are* like real life, but not exactly. In each of his major plays he builds up a particular world which is based in ordinary human experience but which has its own particular powers and limitations. He does this by making each play a poem, that is, a structure of words all interrelated and all tending to a certain order and vision.

In examining each play, then, we must pay the closest attention to how the language works. We may start almost anywhere, since the play is one texture. The following four speeches were selected by a random opening of the text, while these notes were being written:

(1) *Cassius.* I know where I shall wear this dagger then . . . (I,3, 89–)
(2) *Soothsayer.*   . . . Here the street is narrow:
            The throng that follows Caesar at the heels . . .
                                    (II,4, 34–)
(3) *Brutus.* The name of Cassius honours this corruption,
            And chastisement doth therefore hide his head.
                                    (III,3, 15–)
(4) *Pindarus. (Above)* Titinius is enclosed round about . . . (V,3, 28–)

Cassius speaking of suicide as a liberation from tyranny; the Soothsayer planning how to intercept Caesar to warn him; Brutus accusing Cassius of corruption; Pindarus delivering his report on the supposed capture of Titinius. If the theory of a unified but limited world created by the language of the play works, then even such seemingly disparate speeches should have things in common.

And so they have. First and most fundamentally we notice the active energetic use of language: 'strength of spirit', 'shake off'; 'Throng . . . Will crowd a feeble man almost to death'; 'chastisement'; 'make to him on the spur/ Yet he spurs on . . . He's ta'en! And, hark! They shout for joy!' Pressure and anxiety are in all the speeches and the pressure is that of politics and warfare; 'bondage', 'tyrants', images of prisons; crowds 'of senators, of praetors, common suitors'; the stress and opposition of 'honour' with 'corruption'; the galloping horsemen on the battle-field. All this, then, is lively, crackling with energetic excitement; and that excitement, even when personal and emotional, is in the public sphere, is political.

We can go deeper by studying the imagery of the play, by finding out the key words and images by which the main vision of the play is built up. 'Rome' and 'Roman' are the great images of the play and Shakespeare has a certain powerful picture of what this Rome, these Romans are like. Courage, power, and will are reflected in images of metal and of the stones of the great city. Even in our random selection above we have Cassius's dagger, and the stone and metal images of the prison, we have the streets crowded with people, we have the spurs of the horsemen. Master images not found in these quotations are those of gold, which stands ambiguously for both greed and generosity; and blood, a related image which stands for both love and murder. The ambiguity of these master images reflects the central tension of the play, which is also found in Brutus's words about honour and corruption.

Turning to the speech of Antony over Caesar's body we can see a verbal focus for the great central tension of this energetic political play. The word 'ambition' is the thing Caesar stands accused of, the lust for personal power. The word 'honourable' stands at first for the high-minded idealism of Brutus and his fellow-assassins. Both are words of political motivation. Antony, in his speech, gradually but completely reverses the values of the two words so that Caesar, if he was ambitious at all, is felt as a great power of good, having only such ambition as 'did the general coffers fill' and brought pride and wealth to all Romans; while the word 'honourable', turns into a venomous insult, a synonym for treason, malice, and murder. In such ways the tensions of value in the play are reflected by tensions and ambiguities in the words themselves.

Returning to the central images and combining the image of metal to the theme of energy we find, not surprisingly, related images of light and fire, even of electricity, as in the lighting of the storm on the night before Caesar's death, or the static electricity (St. Elmo's Fire) in the seemingly burning hand of the slave. Fire, like the other images of power, also has its ambiguities: it can stand for warmth but it can also destroy: torches from Caesar's funeral pyre light the homes of the conspirators; the fire swallowed by Portia is like the love that kills her. Indeed the whole play could be described in the words of Casca: 'a tempest dropping fire.'

The supernatural in the play mirrors the mood of the whole. There is a sense of terror and awe in the visions of fighting armies, the lionesses in the city, the flaming hands, the 'men, all in fire' who 'walk up and down the streets'; but the terror is stirring and energetic, and there is no real sense of evil in the whole play, a characteristic which it shares with Shakespeare's other Roman plays and which separates them sharply from the four greatest tragedies, *Hamlet*, *Othello*, *King Lear*, and (a play in many other ways very like *Julius Caesar*) *Macbeth*.

There are many other images in *Julius Caesar* which are related to those already examined. We may mention in passing the general use of animal imagery common to most of Shakespeare's plays and here used in relation to the atmosphere we have already described (for instance, Cicero's 'ferret' and 'fiery eyes'; Cassius compared to 'horses hot at hand' by Brutus). A particular image which has caused critics some uneasiness is the hunting imagery used by Antony of the dead Caesar. The extended comparison of Caesar to a dead stag has troubled some readers, but it must be remembered that hunting the stag was a royal sport: energetic, exciting and filled with ceremony. The stag was seen as courageous and noble, a common image for kingship. What more natural than that the sporting Antony should use such an image?

This leads to another point about speech, for although there is a general 'Roman' tone, vocabulary and even rhythm shared by the characters, though they are all to some extent public orators even in their private speeches, yet it must also be observed that they speak in character. To take only the main actors: Caesar's mode of speech is full of authority, proud and commanding; Brutus speaks in measured serious tones, tones of considered judgement (right or wrong) on men and affairs; Cassius's voice is exclamatory, passionate; he is always speaking of his feelings; and Antony, though also passionate, has a more varied tone than any of the others, and, more than any of the others, perhaps that central energy of the play: bright, masculine, lively and compelling.

By the time he wrote *Julius Caesar*, Shakespeare was already the greatest master of dramatic blank verse the world has ever known. In the play he uses his medium with great power but also with a certain restraint. It is notable in the histories which precede *Julius Caesar* that whenever a character has some serious public pronouncement to make the verse becomes more regular and formal, even to some extent more old-fashioned than in other plays Shakespeare wrote about the same time. *Julius Caesar* is a very public play and one which Shakespeare obviously took very seriously, even solemnly. The effect on the verse has been that, though it is powerful and varied in its use of the iambic line, yet it is not as flexible or adventurous, not as close to real speech in its verse rhythms, as other plays of about the same date,—as, say *Twelfth Night*. When we turn to *Hamlet*, the next tragedy he was to write, the difference in flexibility is startling. An easy demonstration of the comparative rigidity of *Julius Caesar* is to look at the number of its lines which are end-stopped,—that is the lines in which the meaning and syntax pause at the end of the line,—and then turn to *Hamlet* and apply the same test; and this is only one test of variation, though a significant one. Here are two speeches which should make the difference clear:

(1) From *Julius Caesar* IV, 1, ll.18–22:

> Octavius, I have seen more days than you;
> And though we lay these honours on this man,
> To ease ourselves of divers slanderous loads,
> He shall but bear them as the ass bears gold,
> To groan and sweat under the business,
>   Either led or driven, as we point the way;
> And having brought our treasure where we will,
> Then take we down his load, and turn him off,
> Like to the empty ass, to shake his ears
> And graze in commons.

(2) From *Hamlet* II, 4, ll.40–48:
>   Such an act
> That blurs the grace and blush of modesty;
> Calls virtue hypocrite; takes off the rose
> From the fair forehead of an innocent love,
> And sets a blister there; makes marriage-vows
> As false as dicers' oaths. O, such a deed
> As from the body of contraction plucks
> The very soul, and sweet religion makes
> A rhapsody of words.

Julius Caesar is a play like the sound of trumpets: a metallic voice on a limited range of notes, but one which stirs the blood with its clear ringing call.

Part 4

Hints for study

The key to the successful study of a Shakespeare play is to remember that it is exactly that, a play. Readers and students who find themselves baffled by Shakespeare, or even bored, are usually put off by the fact that they try to read him as if he were a novelist or a non-dramatic poet; but Shakespeare was writing scripts for a particular company and a particular theatre, and we have these scripts with only the barest stage directions and with no indication, except in the words of the speeches themselves, of how each character is talking.

This makes the reading of a play like *Julius Caesar* a much slower and more concentrated business than the usual sorts of reading prepare us for.

What the reader has to do, if he is to make any sense of the play, is *to put on a production in his head*. He, then, is not a reader, but is a dramatic producer. In the brief summary of the play given above some attempt has been made to show what this means, by suggesting the way people in the play might be talking and the way the action moves along.

In trying to put on a good inner production of any Shakespeare play the script, for all its bareness of stage direction, will help the reader at every turn. Speed, rhythm, expression, even gesture, are built into the living language of the play.

A scene can be read first to find out the main lines of the action. The stage should be visualised, and a rough plan of movement and grouping be worked out. How, for instance, can the funeral oration scene be staged? If the pulpit or speaker's rostrum be placed at the back, up stage, there is the difficulty that the crowd will mostly have their backs to the audience; and it would obviously be ridiculous to have the speakers down stage so that all that we could see of Brutus and Antony would be a back view. Some sort of a slanted arrangement or sidewards arrangement, then, might be a good solution: with the rostrum right or left and slightly up stage so that we could see the faces of the speakers and of at least half of the crowd. This is going to work well when the crowd surge away, first to follow Brutus, leaving Antony and the body of Caesar isolated dramatically. Then, ordered to do so by Brutus, the mob move back grumbling to surround Antony in a rather menacing ring. Later when Antony works them up to rebellion and they start to rush away twice, only to have him call them back, this will give an exciting wavelike rushing to and fro, leading up to their final swarming away carrying the coffin. Antony can then move slowly down centre stage: the man who has let loose the storm now seen in quiet contrasting isolation, rather tired perhaps but with a fierce satisfaction on his face:

'Now let it work . . .'

To make out the finer points of action it is necessary to study each speech in terms of character and of the interaction of character; because, not only should one be able to visualise and hear each speaker in action, but also to imagine how those who are not speaking are reacting to what is being said. At this stage the reader of the play is faced with the formidable task of being all the people in the play at the same time! Even minor parts must be studied. What sort of men are the First, Second, Third, and Fourth Citizens? Where are they going to stand among the crowd, or should they be put in a group together where the audience can see and hear them particularly well? Such problems can be challenging and trying to solve them can bring the whole scene to life.

Another way of reading the play, after a general realisation has been mapped out, will be found to be the best way of studying character. In this approach the reader imagines that he has been given one or other of the major parts, and prepares a set of detailed scene notes for the acting of that part. Given the role of Cassius to 'play' the reader, in an even more personal way than the producer, must work out problems of feeling and motivation, of expression and delivery. Say you are planning the part of Brutus and have to decide how to speak the soliloquy 'It must be by his death . . .' at the beginning of II,1. Are you calm or agitated? Do you stand still or move about as you speak? Do you go through the arguments in a measured rational way, or do you use pauses, and, if so, where? On this interpretation should depend the whole of the development of the part of Brutus throughout the rest of the play. The speech is vital as it gives us the private mind of Brutus for the first time.

A student coming to the play for the first time and with little experience of live theatre may find this task of interpreting a script, of bringing it to life in the imagination, a daunting prospect. An alternative which can help is to try to imagine it, not on the stage, but on film. The task is the same, *a realisation* of action and character, but there can be few students who are not intimately familiar with the way a film works, while many have never had the chance to see live theatre, not to speak of Shakespearean productions. So it may be that they will find the thought of inventing a film of *Julius Caesar* less daunting than that of imagining a theatre production.

Theatre is a communal art which implies a company of actors with their producer and helpers, and also an audience. Another excellent way of lessening the difficulties of realising the play is group study and group reading. Simply for a number of people who have read the play to discuss together how a scene should go on is often a rewarding and exciting experience. To prepare together a dramatic reading of scenes or of the whole play is even better. To put on a real production of scene or play is clearly best of all. Remembering that Shakespeare's own theatre had almost no scenery and only a few touches of Roman costume and a few fairly simple props, an amateur dramatic group should have enough confidence in the power of the words to put on a production with the minimum of technical fuss. Get pace, action, grouping, movement, characterisation, and speech right and the play will work.

Watching a staging or a filming of the play can also be a help to understanding; particularly if it is followed by a discussion of the *way* it was done, and of any particular failures or successes in the production. To see *any* Shakespeare acted or to listen to a good recording will bring his sort of drama alive in the mind.

It has been pointed out that *Julius Caesar* belongs to several interlocking clusters of Shakespearean plays. If possible the more advanced student should read through the histories, particularly the second group of four: *Richard II, Henry IV*, Parts 1 and 2, and *Henry V*; also the Roman Plays *Antony and Cleopatra*, and *Coriolanus* and, if possible, the Tragedies and Problem Plays especially *Hamlet* and *Macbeth*. Plays of other periods on themes of power and war, such as Shaw's *Caesar and Cleopatra* or *St. Joan*, or Brecht's *Mother Courage*, can also provide comparisons to sharpen the awareness of what Shakespeare is doing and how he sets about it. Indeed even novels and films on politics and power will prove useful in this way.

All these are living methods of doing the only worthwhile thing: bringing the play alive in the imagination and making it one's own.

The English audiences of Shakespeare's day had an enormous appetite for fine language and much of the pleasure they derived from the plays was this delight in words. Shakespeare's language has certain difficulties of meaning for the twentieth century English speaker, and any serious student of the play, as part of the study of the text, should make sure that he is aware of the meanings of all words, phrases, and images used. It is a great help to have, as the first text for study, a copy of the play, like the excellent Signet Classic Edition, which gives all difficult meanings at the foot of the page on which they occur.

Shakespeare is easily learnt off by heart: the rhythm, energy, and colour of the speeches often makes them stick in the mind, even if the hearer or reader is not trying to learn them. It is far less fashionable than it used to be to learn by heart, but it must be said that the lasting pleasure and deep knowledge which come from an exact personal possession of a writer's words is not only invaluable in examinations but is a treasure that can last a lifetime. Learn what strikes you most, what moves you most, what interests you most. Make it your own.

Little has been said, so far, about the use of critical studies in understanding the play, but you will have noticed that reference has been made to other commentaries and articles. What should be said is that the reading of criticism comes only after the text has been personally explored at least once. Make the play your own and then use the critics to deepen and widen your experience of it.

However, once the reader's own vision of the play has begun to form, the work of the best critics can help him to make sense of it, and to bring it to life. There is a selected reading list at the end of this book.

Essays and examinations

Finally a few words on writing about *Julius Caesar*, or any other Shakespearean play, for essay or examination.

If a student has managed to make the play his own in the ways suggested above, he will have plenty to say; but he may not be too sure how to organise his knowledge and ideas.

Bear in mind that the play is like a living thing: everything in it is connected to everything else in various ways. Try to show in your answering some of the ways in which these connections work. To do this it is necessary to select, arrange, and illustrate. In selecting show that you are aware of the main aspects of the play, action, character, theme, language, dramatic impact.

Any question or essay topic will be focussed on one or more of these. For instance:

Discuss the view that *Julius Caesar* 'declines in tension and interest after Act III' (*action and structure*);
Consider the importance of Cassius in the play (*character*);
How does Shakespeare build his picture of Rome in the play and what effect has this vision on the play? (*theme and language*);
Consider the variety and effect of events in Brutus's tent (*dramatic impact*).

Now the main thing to remember is what was said earlier about interconnection. To take the character of Cassius: the answer to such a question should show not only the sort of man Shakespeare has given us, but also how he builds up this man in terms of speech and action; and again the effect that Cassius has on the play as a whole: how he causes the events, how he interacts and contrasts with others, how the colour of his personality affects the whole atmosphere of the play. So each approach is a door into one's knowledge of the play as a whole.

It would obviously be impossible to say everything about Cassius, for instance, without writing a sizable book; so, in an examination, selection is of the utmost importance. Make a few key points; link them strongly together; illustrate them with detail—Cassius as villain in the beginning, and as hero at the end; how he works on Brutus and how Brutus masters and dooms him; the calculating thinker who is also a passionate man, angry and affectionate. Short quotations to show these things, or at any rate direct reference to scenes, speeches, or images. A good detailed reference or paraphrase, by the way, is better than an inaccurate quotation. Do not quote unless you are sure of the words; instead, say in your own way how the speech works.

If you always try to link together the different approaches to the play you will avoid those dull answers which show no real understanding of how the play works; those bad answers on character which merely list qualities; and those bad answers on plot which only retell weakly the outline of events. Action comes from character and both come from the way language is used; the study of any of these must be the study of all of them.

Part 5

Suggestions for further reading

Useful editions of the play

The Signet Classic Shakespeare, edited by William and Barbara Rosen, New American Library, New York, 1963
The New Cambridge Shakespeare, edited by J. Dover Wilson, Cambridge University Press, London, 1949
The New Penguin Shakespeare, edited by Norman Sanders, Penguin Books, Harmondsworth 1967
The New Arden Shakespeare, edited by T.S. Dorsch, Methuen and Co., London, 1955

Background

BENTLEY, GERALD E.: *Shakespeare: A Biographical Handbook*, Yale University Press, New Haven, 1961. This gives the plain facts.
BRADBROOK, M.C.: *Elizabethan Stage Conditions*, Cambridge University Press, Cambridge, 1932. This tells how the plays were staged and acted.
BROWN, IVOR: *Shakespeare*, Collins, London, 1949. Imaginative, factual and lively.
BURGESS, ANTHONY: *Shakespeare*, Jonathan Cape, London, 1970. Personal and idiosyncratic; worth arguing with; beautifully illustrated.
CHAMBERS AND WILLIAMS: *A Short Life of Shakespeare*, Oxford University Press, London, 1933. This also gives the plain facts.
HALLIDAY, F.E.: *The Life of Shakespeare*, Penguin Books, Harmondsworth, 1966. A sound recreation of the man and his times.
RIGHTER, ANNE: *Shakespeare and the Idea of a Play*, Chatto and Windus, London, 1962. Shows Shakespeare's changing attitudes to the theatre.
SMITH, IRWIN: *Shakespeare's Globe Playhouse*, Constable and Co. Ltd., London, 1961. Describes the buildings and their effect on the drama.
TILLYARD, E.M.W.: *The Elizabethan World Picture*, Chatto and Windus, London, 1943. Gives the religious, philosophical and political background.

WILLIAMS, R.: *Drama in Performance*, C.A. Watts, London, New Edition, 1968. A general treatment of the plays as theatre down the ages.

WILSON, J.D.: *Life in Shakespeare's England*, Penguin Books, Harmondsworth, 1944. A rich scrapbook of quotations from books and papers of Shakespeare's time.

Criticism

BONJOUR, ADRIEN: *The Structure of 'Julius Caesar'*, Liverpool University Press, Liverpool, 1958. Tells how the play is constructed.

BRADLEY, A.C.: *Shakespearean Tragedy*, Macmillan, London, 1904. The introduction compares *Julius Caesar* to other tragedies.

DOBREE, BONAMY (EDITOR): *Shakespeare, the Writer and his Work*, Longmans, London, 1964. Short clear essays on all the plays.

CHARLTON, H.B.: *Shakespearean Tragedy*, Cambridge, Cambridge University Press, 1966. Gives different attitudes to Julius Caesar, which is treated mainly as a history play.

CHARNEY, MAURICE: *Shakespeare's Roman Plays*, Harvard University Press, Cambridge, Mass., 1961

CLEMEN, WOLFGANG: *The Development of Shakespeare's Imagery*, Methuen, London, 1951. Good on the language.

GRANVILLE-BARKER, HARLEY: *Prefaces to Shakespeare*, Vol. II, Princeton University Press, Princeton, New Jersey, 1947. The finest treatment of *Julius Caesar* as a play.

KNIGHT, G. WILSON: *The Imperial Theme*, Methuen, London, 1951 and *The Wheel of Fire*, Methuen, London, 1949. On imagination and language.

LERNER, LAURENCE (EDITOR): *Shakespeare's Tragedies*, Penguin Books, Harmondsworth, 1963. A useful anthology of essays.

MCCALLUM, M.W.: *Shakespeare's Roman Plays and their Background*, Macmillan, London, 1910. A thorough study.

PALMER, JOHN: *Political Characters of Shakespeare*, Macmillan, London, 1945.

SCHANZER, ERNEST: *The Problem Plays of Shakespeare*, Routledge and Kegan Paul, London, 1963

SPURGEON, CAROLINE: *Shakespeare's Imagery*, Cambridge University Press, Cambridge, 1935. A careful analysis of certain uses of words and images.

TRAVERSI, D.A.: *Shakespeare, The Roman Plays*, Hullis and Carter, London, 1963. A good scene by scene treatment.

VAN DOREN, MARK: *Shakespeare*, Henry Holt and Co., New York, 1939. Short essays on each play.

The author of these notes

SEÁN LUCY is Professor of Modern English in University College, Cork (The National University of Ireland). After graduating in Cork he taught for eight years in England before returning to work in the English Department in UCC. His publications include *T.S. Eliot and the Idea of Tradition* (1960; New York, 1961), he has edited *Love Poems of the Irish* (1967), *Five Irish Poets* (1970), and *Irish Poets in English* (1973). His poems, short stories and critical articles have been published in Ireland, England, France, Denmark, the USA and Canada; and he has broadcast or had his work presented by Radio Telifis Eireann, the British Broadcasting Corporation and Dansk Forefatherforening.

Shakespeare Criticism in three volumes:
 1623–1850, edited by D. Nichol Smith (All Oxford University
 1919–1935, edited by Anne Bradby   Press, London, respec-
 1935–1960, edited by Anne Ridler   tively 1916, 1936, and 1963)
Many articles in *Shakespeare Quarterly* (New York), and *Shakespeare
Survey* (Cambridge).

The sources

BULLOUGH, GEOFFREY: *Narrative and Dramatic Sources of Shakespeare*,
 Vol. V, Routledge and Kegan Paul, London, 1964
SPENSER, T.J.B.: *Shakespeare's Plutarch*, Penguin Books, Harmonds-
 worth, 1964